Divine Ladies in America

Kyra Belán

Astarte Books

Selected Books by Kyra Belán:

Madonnas From Medieval to Modern (Parkstone, 2001)
The Virgin in Art (Barnes and Noble Books 2006)
Lucid Future (novel, CreateSpace 2014)
Earth, Myths, and Ecofeminist Art (CreateSpace 2015)

Divine Ladies in America

Cultural Icons for the New Millennium

Kyra Belán

ISBN: 0578175398

ISBN 13: 9780578175393

Astarte Books
www.kyrabelan.com

Acknowledgement

My thanks to Charles Martin for his patience and understanding, and to my friends that have supported my views for many years. My gratitude to Our Lady of Guadalupe, the people of the Southern US, the people of the city of New York, the people of the city of Nashville, the people of the great state of Arizona, and the people of the awesome state of Florida.

To Tara and Maya

Author's Note

This book is about the inclusive spirituality that pervades America. This spiritual
energy flows like the oceans of the blue planet that grants us our lives.
This spirituality recognizes the divine in women, the Tao, the Chi, and the Shakti
energies within our living planet Gaia; it connects us to the ancient matriarchal myths
that have always existed alongside the dominant male centered spirituality.

Illustrations

Figure 1. Lady Sphinx, painting, copyright 2014 Kyra Belán (back cover)

Figure 2. Mother of Willendorf, digital art, copyright 2014 Kyra Belán

Figure 3. Guadalupe, digital art, copyright 2014 Kyra Belán

Figure 4. Lady Liberty VII, digital art, copyright 2014 Kyra Belán

Figure 5. Goddess Athena, drawing, copyright 2014 Kyra Belán

Figure 6. Isis of Florida, mixed media, copyright 2014 Kyra Belán

Figure 7. Tara, digital art, copyright 2014 Kyra Belán

Figure 8. Lakshmi, panting, copyright 2014 Kyra Belán

Figure 9. Coatlicue, digital art, copyright 2014 Kyra Belán

Figure 10. Magna Mater, digital art, copyright 2014 Kyra Belán

Figure 11. Akua Ba, digital art, copyright 2014 Kyra Belán

Figure 12. Juno, digital art, copyright 2014 Kyra Belán

Figure 13. Goddess Trinity, digital art, copyright 2014 Kyra Belán

Contents

2.

Introduction

United States of America is an amalgamation of many cultures. This great country is a multi-layered tapestry of civilizations that originated all over the world and have converged to form this awesome country. Contemporary American culture grants each individual with the freedom of spiritual expression. American people experiment with their spirituality in a variety of ways. This civilization, inherited predominantly from the European West, is currently undergoing the most radical metamorphosis since Pagan Europe lost its innocence and religious freedom to the Christian dogma during the early centuries of the Middle Ages.

Conventional spirituality of the United States is usually connected to the mainstream Christianity, which was brought in by the original settlers who relocated to America to escape their own religious persecution in the old world. The founders of America believed in their religious freedom, and they made sure that the separation of state and church was written into the constitution. They lived during the Age of Reason, and consequently many called themselves Deists: they believed in a Creator, however did not assign any particular religious beliefs or gender to this Deity. Even though American religiosity is largely derivative of Christianity, other significant factors make this spiritual heritage a blend that consists of myths from Ancient Europe, Africa, Asia, and the Native American cultures. Originally, Christianity itself, the dominant religion of America, was an amalgamation of several earlier, ancient myths. It has gone through a variety of transformations and is still a work in progress, adjusting itself to match the expectations and needs of its followers.

Spirituality that sprang out of a patriarchal social order values men more than it values women, and traditional Christian dogma is not an exception. Two thousand years of a patriarchal order supported by a male dominated religion, conditioned women to accept secondary roles within the traditional Christian Church. Yet the gradual inclusion of women into the work force, politics, and economic development of American culture during the nineteenth and twentieth centuries created a social movement that is changing our society in a radical fashion. Women are no longer the silent gender that does not participate in the spiritual discourse. During the last quarter of the twentieth century women have been significantly altering American culture, and this powerful female undercurrent is fueling the process of re-evaluating, challenging, and modifying the dominant culture and its established myths and archetypes. Feminist thinking has changed the way we understand psychology, philosophy, sociology, the sciences, and the arts. This change is affecting the way our religious myths and archetypes are perceived and interpreted.

Even the misogynist version of Christian religion that dominated Europe for nearly two thousand years always contained an occult version of the ancient Mother Goddess. Next to the patriarchal male God there was the Mother of God; she was the feminine face of God within the psyche of the population, in spite of the prevalence of female oppression. The images of the sacred feminine, inherited from the ancient world and the Native cultures affected the spirituality of American people and paved the way for the acceptance of the divine female archetypes within contemporary culture and social media. Currently we possess a heritage upon which a society that could value and respect feminine spirituality as much as it values and respects the masculine, could form. New interpretations of spirituality allow American women to live without being diminished by the traditional interpretation of a God, without the perpetuation of the misogynist legends propagated by the male writers of the past. As a nation, we are in the process of spiritual development that allows us to visualize the divine beings according to a variety of cultural legends: as a male, a female, as a form of energy, or as an abstract concept.

The female archetypes of the divine have been around in America during its entire existence as a colony and a country. Some were adopted from the Native American religions, other brought in by the settlers from Europe, Africa, Asia, or even Australia. During the last four decades, people have been incorporating traditionally feminine values of caring, interconnectedness, peace, and ecological concerns into the mainstream of American cultural discourse. The inclusion of these values into the structure of a post-modern society is impacting our personal views. People of the twenty-first century are adopting a feminized value system. Consequently, there is a longing to achieve a balanced model of spirituality that matches the new social paradigm. The infusion of the sacred feminine into American society is of a direct benefit to both genders, as it encourages flexibility within the gender-defined roles, and promotes shared responsibility of caring for our children.

Recent research into the prehistoric, Old European, Native American, African, Asian, Australian, and other world cultures by the archeologists, anthropologists, sociologists, and art historians has unearthed new evidence of the universality of the religions of the Great Mother God on our planet. It has been discovered that many cultures -- including the prehistoric, ancient, and the Native American -- successfully maintained matriarchal societies that supported female spiritual practices for many thousands of years. A number of these matriarchal cultures have survived the impact of patriarchy and still exist within the dominator societies. There is a commonality of characteristics which determine a typical matriarchal culture: the supreme Creator or

God is represented in a woman's form, the societies are matrilineal regarding the inheritance of lands, titles, clans, and the naming of children. The males, however, are not oppressed and have equal rights with women; they fully participate in the cultural dialogue, occupy prestigious leadership positions, and are included together with the women in all the aspects of religious rituals and worship, although women priests may at times dominate. These social structures may be ruled by the following: a matriarch, a priestess-queen, two priestesses-queens, a royal couple, a male ruler, or a tribal council usually representative of both female and male genders. The class hierarchy within these societies is minimized, and the distribution of wealth is spread more equitably among the people. When division of labor exists according to gender, work done by females is respected as much as the labor generated by the males. Perhaps the most critical characteristic of these prehistoric, ancient or contemporary matriarchal cultures is that they are predominantly peaceful; wars and killings are discouraged within these societies. This particular characteristic of matriarchal structures has become an important issue for contemporary research. Americans oppose the idea of war, and believe that military conflict is justifiable only as a defense mechanism. American public also regards human life as precious.

Matriarchal societies, still in existence in isolated pockets within contemporary patriarchal cultures worldwide, confirm that these cultures flourished in the past. We must remember that the prehistoric and ancient matriarchal societies had a much longer existence on this planet than the comparatively recent patriarchal cultures that followed them. The dating of the origins of matriarchal societies varies, but according to several sources, including the famous books on the subject by Marija Gimbutas, they existed as far back as 30,000 B C E. As research continues, some scientists and archeologists entertain the probability that the presence of matriarchies can be traced as far back as 800,000 B C E. The earliest patriarchies were established around 5,000 B C E. These patriarchies, during their early stages of existence, combined their dominator characteristics with the components from their matriarchal predecessors. It took many centuries for these societies to become fully male dominated, war oriented, and hierarchical. This process of andro-centricity, which ultimately excluded women from all decision-making and cultural discourse, and, in extreme cases, deprived them of all human rights, was nearly completed about two thousand years ago. At that time, a new dominant religion, deprived of the powerful and compassionate Mother Goddess, was generated to support this new social order, which depended for its existence on the free labor and procreation abilities of the disempowered female gender. But was this new patriarchal religion originally deprived of the divine feminine? Although official religious dogma will make you believe that this was so, recent research disputes this fact.

According to the current research by the feminist scholars of both genders, Christianity was more equitable to women in its formative stages. When it first arrived in Europe via Ancient Rome, it was fundamentally a different religion since its deity was interpreted as having both male and female characteristics. From the old Goddess-centered religions, it adopted the concept of a divine trinity. The original trinity, female in matriarchal times, represented the three aspects of a God as a woman: the Virgin God as the Creative Force, the Mother God whose primary function was that of the Nurturer, and the Crone, who was the personification of

Wisdom and Transformation. This triple nature of the Great Goddess was transplanted into Christianity via previous mixed gender trinities of earlier patriarchies, like that of the divine family of Isis, Osiris, and Horus of the ancient Egyptians. Also, at the beginning of Christianity, the triple divinity was not defined as only masculine. The early church fathers had different interpretations for the triune nature of their supreme being, and the three aspects of the new Christian God were frequently subjected to heated discussions and interpretations among the clergy leaders and the dominant male followers. The early Christian God, based on the Old Testament, was seen as having two aspects: a male called Jehovah or Yahweh, and a female called Sophia or Wisdom. At the onset of Christianity, The Holy Ghost or Spirit, the third aspect of the future all male trinity was not defined in terms of gender. Some early Christian sects saw the Holy Spirit as the female component of their triune God, but later it was re-established as the male form of the divine, an idea that was ultimately adopted as the official dogma; yet it is still visually represented by a dove, an ancient symbol for many female divinities. When Mary the Mother of God was incorporated into the Christianity during the second and third centuries, she was equated with the Great Goddess Isis, whose religion dominated the ancient world.

The long history of the religion of Mother God Isis is complex; her worship lasted for over four thousand years. She presented a major threat to the new Christian faith up to sixth century CE, but the introduction of the Virgin Mary as the Mother of God established Christianity as the dominant cult of Europe. At that time Mary was believed to be a part of the familiar trinity of God the Father, God the Mother, and God the Son, identical to the trinity of the Isian cult of the Egyptians and of the ancient world. However, to her ancient worshipers, Isis ultimately encompassed in herself all the gods and goddesses of Egypt as an omnipotent creator; therefore, she was the primal divine manifestation. Goddesses Hathor and Sekhmet, her predecessors and contemporaries, were seen as also her aspects. In view of these facts, it was natural for the early Christians to interpret Holy Virgin Mary as the Great Mother Goddess, and as the syncretic Great Isis. During medieval times in Europe the worship of Mary as the Mother Goddess continued, and was tolerated by and even condoned by the church fathers. This unofficial belief was helpful to them: the presence of this feminized version of Christianity helped establish it as the prevalent religion of Europe. During the Renaissance, a period that spanned roughly between the fourteenth and sixteenth centuries, the powerful church fathers declared that the Holy Virgin Mary was not a Goddess, but only a vessel for the birth of her divine male child, a necessary pre-requisite that allowed his incarnation to occur. This declaration excluded official Marian worship; nevertheless, the public continued to worship her, so the cult of the Virgin Mary continued. Numerous miraculous apparitions of Mother Mary increased in Europe and expanded to other continents, including the Americas. These apparitions still continue into the twenty-first century, and constitute the biggest spiritual phenomenon of our times, occurring with frequency and regularity all over the planet. Due to the acceleration in the development of communications technologies, we have become aware of the frequency of these sightings.

Mary the Mother of God is not the only legendary Goddess of contemporary America. The Native American culture, long suppressed, is currently emerging as a new force, fueling interest in the worship of a compassionate Mother God, not unlike Mother Mary. Most Native American cultures were matriarchal, and most still are; therefore, they perceive planet Earth as a manifestation of the Great Mother, the creator and nurturer of all life. This reverence for Mother Earth is echoed within the proponents of the new scientific movement, known as the Gaia Theory, named after the original Mother God of Ancient Greece. According to this theory, our planet functions as a living organism, self-generating and regenerating. Humanity is seen as an integral part of the planet. In the age of American ecological movements, inspired by feminist theorists, radical change in the treatment of Gaia is essential to the continuation of life upon this planet, and the survival of humanity. However, the implementation of this agenda requires a specific mindset by the majority of the world's population. It is imperative that feminine values of the matriarchal and Native American societies are integrated into the new upcoming social order, defined by Riane Eisler as the *partnership model.*

The descendants of the people who came to America from various regions of Africa are the ancestors of the African American population. These people, originally brought in as slaves, carried with them their local traditions that included powerful goddesses. Due to the oppression by the mainstream patriarchal culture, these first African Americans had to hide their spirituality as they were forcefully converted into Christianity by the dominator culture. Many secretly continued to practice their original beliefs, and celebrated their Goddesses and Gods, cleverly disguised as Mother Mary, Jesus, and various Christian saints. Currently, there is an increase in the interest in African cultures. Syncretic religions of this country, such as Voodoo and Santeria, are based on African spirituality and rituals, as well as on Christian faith, and are currently practiced by a substantial segment of the population of African, Afro-Latin and Latin descent.

Another culturally distinct wave of people arrived to America via Asia, from countries such as China, Korea, Japan, Cambodia, and Viet Nam. They brought with them the worship of one particular Goddess that has similarities with the Christian Mother of God, and is also the Great Bodhisattva within Buddhist religion: the Goddess of Mercy and Compassion, Kwan Yin or Guan Yin. This Goddess, like Mary, is perceived as a benevolent divinity that radiates the purest form of love for humanity. As the Bodhisattva, she is an evolved spirit who, because of her devotion to her people, choses to direct her divine powers toward the earthly realm in order to help humanity. The popularity of Guan Yin among the Americans may have been triggered by the dissemination of eastern spirituality and philosophy during the nineteen sixties.

India, an eastern country that contributed to the revival of female spirituality in America, has worshiped the divine feminine on an equal basis with the male gods in the past, and still does today. When India adopted its patriarchal structure, based on gender oppression and a rigid cast system, it unsuccessfully attempted to erase the divine feminine out of its religions and mythologies. Yet the Goddess came back to assume her powerful role within the rich and complex structure of the myths, rituals, legends, and philosophy of Hinduism. While the oppression of female gender is still a problem within India, women have been able to break out of patriarchal restrictions and achieve high political and religious status due to the presence of the divine feminine within their culture.

Another popular Asian-American Goddess is known as Tara. She is the ancient supreme Mother of the Tibetans and is also the Mother of all the Buddhas. She is believed to be the bringer of miracles, health and healing, and is worshiped in numerous Asian countries. People of Asian descent that have relocated to America brought their devotion to Tara with them. Neo-Pagans, followers of New Age movement, and feminist Americans also include her in their rituals, prayers, spirituality, and enjoy displaying her images within their public and private dwellings.

According to recent surveys in the news and on television, nearly forty percent of Americans believe in more than one religious philosophy and draw from a variety of spiritual sources to complete their personal beliefs. It is apparent that diverse forms of spirituality in America are on the rise, and female faces of god are emerging. Several reasons are contributing to this re-emergence of the divine feminine: the equalization of women within our society; a strong interest in alternative philosophies that embrace a compassionate and peaceful way of life; the discovery of the new archeological evidence of the existence of matriarchal societies that functioned successfully for extended periods of time; and the possibility of a partnership society that may evolve out of our current social system. This latter model, according to the sociologist and futurist Riane Eisler and her followers, is already replacing the old dominator order. Perhaps the strongest motivating force is the desire within the human consciousness to find a personal, loving, and compassionate God through the visualization of a Supreme Deity as the All Loving Mother.

On a more intimate level, for many women and men who are not religious, the re-discovery and revival of the history of woman-centered religions, archetypes, myths, rituals, and matriarchal social systems is important due to the popularity of the Gaia Theory and the rise of the process philosophy which proposes that the dynamic nature of existence should be the locus of spiritual philosophies. The more inclusive image of a supreme being represents a complete vision of the history of humankind and opens the possibility of a gender-balanced and eco-conscious society. The myths and the archetypes of the feminine are relevant to the events of our contemporary lives and are accepted by humans on many levels. This vast heritage of female spirituality comprises a large portion of art and artifacts dispersed across the globe: archeological sites, museums, public places, temples, churches, and private collections. Along with these priceless objects of high art, a constant stream of reproductions of the images of the divine feminine is being generated for popular consumption. Thus, mass-produced, vernacular and *kitsch* art adorns private family dwellings of those who embrace an unstructured, non-dogmatic, dynamic, philosophical, and personal spirituality. The biggest need for the reinstatement of Mother Goddess within America is due as much to the lay society as to the rise in inclusive spirituality. The craving of the souls for the feminine myths and the faces of God is engendered by the desire to equalize the status of women within the patriarchal misogynist religions, and to bring the feminine values that promote peace, equality, and reverence for all living beings into the mainstream culture, as America enters a new phase of its socio-spiritual development.

This book examines some of the feminine archetypes, legends, and mythologies that have captured the imaginations of people in America, and about which the Americans are passionate. These myths and symbols are analyzed, elucidating their matriarchal origins and their infusion into the mainstream culture. They are a part of our popular culture, interwoven into its social fabric. The American people are discovering and experiencing these symbols, archetypes, and myths of the divine feminine at an unprecedented level. The material in this book attempts to clarify and expand upon the knowledge and understanding of sacred femininity within the diversity of America of the new millennium.

3.

1

Our Lady of Guadalupe, Goddess of the Americas

Our Lady of Guadalupe is a powerful example of a divine woman in America. She manifests herself within contemporary American culture in numerous ways. Pope John Paul II declared her the patron of Mexico and the Americas; her sacred image appears in churches and cathedrals throughout the nation, including the renowned St. Peter's Cathedral located in the middle of uptown Manhattan in New York City. The original image of Our Lady of Guadalupe, believed by many to be the ultimate miraculous Christian icon, is called the *tilma*. Housed in the famous cathedral, dedicated to Our Lady of Guadalupe and located in Mexico City, it is the center of a year round pilgrimages from every direction within the Americas, and from all over the world. This Black Madonna, according to the testaments of her worshipers, generates miracles that surpass in frequency those of her other sacred locations, including the Lourdes of France. The replicas of Our Lady of Guadalupe, available due to popular demand, include a huge array of statuary, two-dimensional works such as murals, paintings, and drawings, and various *kitsch* items such as clocks, wall hangings, key chains, hats, and tee shirts sold at the stores and supermarkets across the country and online. The popular seven-day candles that carry her image are usually available at every neighborhood's grocery or drug store. She is venerated by the Latin population in America, which extends throughout most of the southern states, the west, and the east coast. La Guadalupe entered the United States via Mexico, our neighbor with whom we share a substantial amount of common border. What is significant about this Christian Mother of God is that she happens to be a *syncretic* Goddess, as she also represents the loving Mother of the Native American population, Goddess Tonantzin of the Aztecs and the mother of the Aztec God of Truth. Early on in the history of Mexico she became associated with the Mother of God of the religion of the *conquistadores,* who also had a son.

Special masses are held for her at many churches in America to celebrate the date of her first miraculous apparition in Mexico City in 1531. They usually take place on the twelfth of December of each year. A mass that is dedicated to the Virgin of Guadalupe includes a re-enactment, narrated in Spanish, of the story of her apparitions to Juan Diego, the native son of Mexico, and is designed to attract predominantly Latino/a worshipers. According to the myth, each time the Virgin Mary/Aztec Goddess Tonantzin appeared to Juan Diego, she spoke *Nahuatl,* the language that he could understand. He did not speak Spanish, the language of the *conquistadores* who subjugated the Aztecs a decade earlier. The fact that she spoke their native language indicated to the Aztec and *Mestizo* population that the Great Mother indeed was their indigenous Goddess. Because of the sacred intervention by the Lady, the conquered and the conquerors were able to peacefully blend into a new race, *la raza* of Mexico. Within the Latin population, *La Morenita* or the Black Madonna of the Americas is believed to be the expression of the best of both cultures. Most importantly, *La Guadalupe* is perceived as the loving Mother of all the people of Hispanic descent, the one to whom they pray for personal reasons. Believed to perform powerful miracles, she is often summoned to cure terminal illnesses, to grant secret desires and intimate wishes, and to right all the wrongs. Many of her altars are set up inside private residencies where she is celebrated as a personal Redeemer. Many carry her card size images in their wallets, alongside their credit or debit cards. Hand painted, sculpted, and mass produced images of the Guadalupe are often displayed on the dashboards of their vehicles. Her religion is a blend of Native and Western theologies, and is the main reason why Mexico has successfully formed its culture, an amalgamation of the Native Aztec civilization and that of the Spanish invaders from the Old World.

The Lady of Guadalupe is immensely important to the Christianity of the Americas. Out of over twenty-one thousand recorded apparitions of *La Virgen María,* the Guadalupan vision is the only one that left concrete evidence of her visit, which, after numerous scientific tests and investigations, still stands as the most outstanding physical evidence within the Christian belief system – the *tilma,* an image of *La Virgen* on *a* cloth garment. This article has defied the tests of time, and retains the mystique of an otherworldly, indefinable, yet absolutely physical object. The second most famous miraculous Christian item, the Shroud of Turin, unlike the *tilma,* has enough detractors to cast doubts on its authenticity, and the quality of its image is considerably inferior to that of the *tilma* in terms of its clarity, colors, and details. By leaving such startling evidence, Mary immediately became the most powerful *Evangelist* and *Redeemer* for the Christian Church of the Americas. The complete story of the series of her apparitions is considered by her devotees to be the fifth Gospel of Christianity.

Since Our Lady of Guadalupe spoke to Juan Diego in Nauhatl, she directly addressed the Native population of Mexico and was instantly recognized by the Natives as their own Goddess, the compassionate and all loving Earth Mother

Tonantzin, herself an aspect of the greatest of all the Aztec Gods, Coatlicue. The Goddess Coatlicue, according to the Aztec mythology, is the creator divinity, and the Mother of all the Goddesses and Gods. But for the Spanish, she represented the all loving and compassionate Mother of God, *La Virgen María*. The Virgin of Guadalupe allowed the two races to merge spiritually: the Aztecs were easily converted to Christianity after her apparitions took place in the city of Mexico.

Clearly the theology of the Guadalupan apparitions is about a contact with a powerful female energy, the essence of God the Mother. She identified herself as Tonantzin, who was also the Mother of Tloque Nahuaque or Teotl, the Aztec God of Truth, who was equated with the Christian Jesus in the minds of the population, and the *padres* of the Church encouraged this syncretic perception of their religion at that time. Tonantzin chose to appear to no one else but Juan Diego, an Aztec who spoke only Nahuatl, and did not even understand Spanish. This happened just ten years after the Spanish conquered Tenochtitlán, later to become Mexico City, the capital of Mexico. This miraculous event took place on December the ninth on the hill of Tepeyac, a territory of the Goddess Tonantzín. She was named by the Spanish *La Guadalupe*, maybe because the word Tlecohuatlapcopeuh, meaning in Aztec *The One Who comes from the Region of the Light, like the Fire Eagle*, sounded to them quite similar to the name of the Spanish Virgin of Guadalupe, the miraculous Black Madonna of the European continent. The title seemed right for the Mother God who was seen by the devout as The Woman Clothed with the Sun, a phrase from the Apocalypse that equated her with an archetypal Sun Goddess. The Virgin of Guadalupe is that, too, as an aspect of the omnipotent Creator Goddess Coatlicue, whose immense powers, according to the beliefs of the Aztecs, identify her as the ultimate creator of hundreds of Gods and Goddesses, among them a Sun God and a Moon Goddess. Tonantzín was also worshiped as a Moon Goddess; within Marian Iconography the Moon was closely associated with The Virgin brought in from Europe by the Spanish. Another Aztec word, Tequatlaxupe, may have served as an inspiration for the Spanish name of Guadalupe, and it means *the one who crushes the stone serpent*. This meaning is appropriate to Marian legends, since the Madonna is often represented as standing on a serpent, as the one who conquers all evil. But we must remember that Tonantzín's full Aztec name was Tonantzín Cuahtlalpancihuateotl, or the Lunar Lady and Queen of the Waters, and her principal temple was located near the hill of Tepeyac, next to the village of Cuahtlalpan. The latter term could have been the name that was conveniently transformed by the Christian clergy into Guadalupe, most likely because of the familiar reference to the miraculous Black Madonna of Spain. By appearing to Juan Diego, Our Lady of Guadalupe-Tonantzin restored his dignity as a human being, previously lost to the conquerors, and through him, that dignity was accorded to all the Aztec and Native people whose lives and hopes were thus revitalizes due to the divine presence on the site.

The complete official account of the event is believed to be written by Don Antonio Valeriano several years later, and is called the *Nican Mopohua*. Valeriano was an indigenous pupil of Friar Bernardino de Sabagún, who died in 1548. Even though some years had elapsed, the reliability of the account is high, considering that the traditional books of the Gospels were written seventy or more years after the events of the New Testament initially happened. The Virgin of Guadalupe's request to have her temple build on the site of the old temple dedicated to Tonantzín further reinforced the idea that the old and the new faiths were forever merged together in the new post-conquest land of the Americas.

The story of repeated apparitions and the miracles of *Santa María-Tonantzín* is about the divine intervention: thus, the Great Mother prevented the bloodshed and further destruction of the indigenous civilizations, and induced a state of peaceful coexistence of two disparate cultures, forever fusing them into a new society, a new race, and a new country of the Americas. Each time Guadalupe appeared to Juan Diego, the surrounding environment was miraculously changed, leaving him with a sense of wonder. At the beginning, the humble Aztec was unable to fulfill her requests, since the person that he was supposed to contact, the bishop Juan de Zamárraga, did not believe him till after several miracles materialized, including a sudden cure of Juan Diego's dying uncle. The last miracle, the impression of her image on the *tilma* worn by Juan Diego, totally convinced the bishop and the rest of the community of the miraculous nature of the apparition. Juan Diego himself was unaware of the presence of the image on his *tilma* till the moment he unfolded it in front of the bishop to show him the miraculous flowers that the Holy Virgin asked him to gather on the hill of Tepeyac. Almost immediately the construction of the first of the Guadalupan temples was initiated, and the cult of *Nuestra Senora de Guadalupe* emerged, like a rising sun, illuminating the lives of those in need for miracles and hope.

The history of the *tilma* indicates that it was a part of the traditional indigenous attire made out of a*gave* or *maguey* plants that belong to the cactus family. This kind of fabric usually has a life span of about twenty years. Yet the image of Guadalupe-Tonantzín, imprinted on the *tilma*, is still totally intact after over four hundred and eighty years of existence. This is true in spite of the changes in temperature through the years, the frequent kissing and handling of the image by thousands of hands, and the exposure to the soot of the burning candles. In 1791, after the *tilma* was finally framed, a major accident occurred: two workers spilled some nitric acid onto the *tilma*, which produced only a slight discoloration of the cloth, while the metal frame around the image was destroyed by the acid. Another, even more drastic incident took place in 1921 at the old temple built in Baroque style, when a bomb was stashed inside a flower vase located below the sacred image. The explosion occurred at the end of the mass, damaging the surrounding area, including the marble bas-reliefs on the walls. It also melted a processional cross that was forged out of copper and gold, yet did not damage the sacred image. The *tilma* is now displayed at the new temple, the basilica currently in use by the worshipers to commemorate one more miraculous event – the fact that the explosion and the fire did not destroy it. Today the *tilma* is enclosed under the bulletproof glass for protection against any future accidents.

The miraculous provenance of the *tilma* has been tested numerous times. Perhaps the most definitive scientific investigation took place under the direction of an American scientist and Nobel Prize winner by the name of Richard Kuhn. Kuhn originally hoped to debunk the *tilma*'s otherworldly qualities. However, after investigating the garment in 1936, Kuhn's conclusion was that "the elements that produce the colored patches on the cloth are unknown to all research. Neither

Kyra Belán

mineral, animal, nor vegetable, the image seems to have been painted without any brush or lithographic method."[1] Kuhn and his scientific team also noticed that the angel at Mary's feet, and the golden rays of light that surround and seem to emanate from her body were added later, painted in oil. Her elegant fingers were shortened, as they also were repainted with oil. Unlike other miracle producing relics, this one withstood rigorous investigations, and still sustains the veracity of its otherworldly nature.

According to the popular lore, another peculiarity of the *tilma* is that it seems to represent the sky of the winter solstice on the cape that Our Lady is wearing, coinciding exactly with the time of her miraculous appearances during the month of December of 1531. The same constellations were visible during the morning of December 12, at sunrise, when Juan Diego was showing the cape to the bishop Zamárraga. These include the Boreal Crown constellation above her head, the constellation of Virgo on her chest, the constellation of Leo in the area of her womb, and Orion by her feet. This latter location houses an angel that was painted at a later date. Yet another otherworldly effect of the image is the discovery, around 1948, that in the eyes of the Guadalupe one can detect a reflection of a bearded man, similar to that of Juan Diego. In the last fifteen years, more reflections of people were found in her eyes when the photographs of the details within the irises were magnified with the aid of the computers. Unlike the miraculous durability of the *tilma*, these conclusions may be debatable, in part or as a whole; however, they conclusively prove that the presence of the *tilma* is generating an extensive Marian mythology of the Americas. From an aesthetic point of view, the composition of the image is balanced, if analyzed in terms of the proportions of the golden rule. The golden rule is often used within the fine arts as the ideal way to organize the elements of art into a unified whole.

Indeed the Great Mother is full of surprises, as her *tilma* continues to mystify the scientific community. One of the many scientists that analyzed the *tilma* in the late seventies, Dr. Philip Callahan from Florida State University, declared that there is no human explanation for the creation of the image, and that it is probable that we will never know how it was made.[2] The presence of this level of concrete evidence of the visitations by Guadalupe-Tonantzín is a constant reminder of the presence of the divine feminine. The effects of this powerful presence have not been studied enough to fully comprehend its impact. It is a statement, however, against the outdated values within the patriarchal religious establishment, and promotes an idea of a need for a change within Christianity. It may also convince the Catholic Church to recognize that the feminine divine energy is of enormous benefit to the people of Christian faith. The Christian religious establishment is not willing to eliminate its misogynist stand against women, but women are becoming aware of their theological heritage and the power of female spirituality. It is likely that contemporary Christians, aided by the effects of Guadalupe's mysticism, may force the religious establishment to include into Christianity an official recognition of Mary as not only the Mother of God, but also, like her Son, a Divine Redeemer of humanity. If this takes place, Christianity, a male oriented religion, could become a liberating experience for all. Deeper reverence for Our Lady of Guadalupe may accelerate the healing of the planet, our Mother Earth, and save Christianity from becoming obsolete.

While the Christian *padres* of Mexico believed that the Native American religion that worshiped Tonantzín was eradicated by the new Catholic faith of the conquerors, they were premature in assuming a total victory. Even though the official dogma refuses to mention the syncretism of the Guadalupan beliefs, the Aztec Goddess has become one with the Catholic *Santa María*, amalgamating the two religions forever. The belief in Tonantzín is more widespread and active today than at any other time since the conquest of the territories known today as Mexico. The Guadalupan religion is currently practiced throughout Mexico and in America among the Hispanic populations, not only through the official channels such as church services and home altars, but also through a form of shamanism. The practitioners are women, often the descendants of those who were displaced by the *conquistadores* since the new Christian religion did not permit women to participate in its rituals. The priestesses of the Goddess went underground and continued performing their own rituals in their homes. These women shamans are usually called *curanderas* or *brujas*, psychics who perform a ritual for every possible situation, from a magic spell to a healing ritual, to the delivery of a child. These shamanic women are the neighborhood doctors that the poor people can afford, and they are hired to compliment conventional treatments for the best possible results. Currently, the *brujas* or *curanderas*, highly adaptable to the changing culture, are successfully practicing their craft in America. In fact, this brand of shamanism is moving into the American culture as shamans of Nature Magic, and as a part of the New Age movement, Pagan spirituality, and Goddess worship.

The supreme Goddess of the *brujas* is *La Guadalupe*, the All Powerful One who can achieve anything, and is seen as omnipotent. The Aztec culture's mythology is complex, and Guadalupe has inherited the role of *Tonan*. Her range of powers enables her to promote the health, prosperity, fertility, and happiness of the people, and the entire eco-system. Tonantzín is an aspect of Coatlicue, the Great Mother of all the indigenous Goddesses and Gods, and therefore the omnipotent Creator. Amazingly, this indigenous divinity is triune, and was celebrated as the Creator-Maiden, the Mother-Nurturer and the Wise Woman-Transformer. This female trinity was similar to the trinities of the early Goddesses that the pre-historic and ancient humanity worshipped in Old Europe, Near East, Asia, and other continents. The *brujas* had to disguise the fact that the luminous Tonantzín, Goddess of the Aztec legends and customs, was still the divinity of the people. Therefore, these female shamans of the Goddess looked for and found parallels and similarities within the Christian cult that they could use in order to mask the indigenous connections. Tonantzín-Coatlicue was the creator of the universe, including the stars, Sun, and Moon. Instead of carrying native names of the divinities, the stars became Christian saints and angels, the Moon was seen as *La Virgen María*, and the Sun was often interpreted as her son Jesus who replaced native Quetzalcoatl as a part of the cover-up. In the *Brujería*, the syncretic cult originally practiced as Aztec religion, there was a place of privilege for the souls of the warriors who died in battles and the women who died in childbirth, and this place could be easily equated to Christian paradise. The Christian purgatory, a place for the average sinner's soul, was the equivalent of the Mictlán where most Aztec souls were expected to reside after their transformation into ethereal beings. This zone, together with the nine-layered realm reminiscent of Christian hell, were ruled by the Aztec God Mictlantecuhtli, who reminded the healers-witches or *brujas* of the Christian Satan.[3]

Unlike the hierarchical structure of the patriarchal Christianity, the Aztec religion had a division of labor between the priestesses and priests. The male priesthood was in charge of the many ceremonial functions that usually ended with human sacrificial offerings to the Deities, a symbolic destruction in order to appease and nourish the Gods, while the female priesthood was in charge of the nourishing functions, appropriate to the creators of life. Both functions were deemed necessary for the survival of the Aztec people. The *brujas*, as the new Guadalupan clergy, interpreted the Christian exclusion of women from priesthood as the indicator that, like in the old days, the elaborate public rituals and functions were the domain of the men. However, the women as the nurturers, life givers, and healers, continued to implement the feminine aspects of the rituals in a more private manner. The fact that the ritual of confession was exclusively in the hands of the males was met with resentment and disapproval from these priestesses of the Guadalupan religion. Afraid to resist because if they rebelled, they could have been persecuted and killed, they found a solution. They told their following to confess to the *padres* all their minor and average sins, while the major ones would have to be resolved by the *curanderas* of the *Todopoderosa* - All-Powerful Guadalupe through the intervention of her priestesses. Under the new patriarchal conditions it was not possible for them to establish their own temples, as they would have been severely punished by the fathers for such a transgression. Therefore, the priestesses placed the statues, images, and altars to Guadalupe in the privacy of their own homes. Even the incense that the Christian fathers used for their rituals had to be adopted by the *curanderas*, since the native *copal* became hard to obtain.[4] Eventually the practitioners of the Guadalupan Magic in Mexico and in America developed connections with other spiritual women and men. Thus, they gained access to the herbal knowledge of the tribal shamans such as the Yaqui, as well as those priestesses and priests who practiced the secret knowledge of the Wicca, Voodoo, Spiritualism, Santería, and other non-mainstream ancient religions that are currently practiced.

The nurturing and healing powers of *La Lupe* are believed by her followers to be omnipresent. Her official websites, sanctioned by the Catholic Church, encourage the worshipers to send an email with a request or a petition. This completes the full circle of the Guadalupan worship in the lives of the people of the Americas. The compassionate Mother-Redeemer is always available to ease the pain and struggles of her people, and to fulfill their wishes. She can give hope and power to those who are dispossessed: usually they are the women, the persecuted, and the working people not born to privileges. Those people are the opposite of the rulers and the wealthy of the world. But to gain favors from Guadalupe one must be coming from the light, and Guadalupe herself is that light in her aspects of the Sun and the Moon Goddess. Her followers must help and support others, and contribute to the well being of Mother Earth; the practitioners and the priestesses of *Tonantzín* practice only white magic. The followers, under the influence of the *brujas* or shamans, learn how to participate in the rituals and to re-create them on their own. La Guadalupe possesses a huge array of personal rituals, magic, and spells that she, through her shamans, can teach her beloved people. But the *curanderas* and the followers no longer use the Aztec calendar. The Church *padres* have performed a thorough job in suppressing it, yet some vestiges of the indigenous calendar are still imbedded into the Guadalupan holidays. Originally, Tonantzín's principal festivity was celebrated on December the ninth, which is also the day of the first Marian apparition on the hill of Tepeyac. This date originally was proclaimed by the Church as an official holiday to honor *La Lupe*, but in the middle of the eighteenth century the fathers decided to eradicate this calendrical connection to *Tonan*, and changed the date to December the twelfth. Both dates are within the range of the Winter Solstice, and are close to Christmas, another date that was conveniently adjusted by Christianity centuries ago to make itself compatible with the earlier Pagan rituals to celebrate their Goddess and God on or around the Solstice. The priestesses of Tonan-Guadalupe, however, still celebrate the ninth of December as her main festivity in spite of the change made to the official calendars by the Christian fathers.

Every year on the twelfth day of December, the official Marian holiday, a colorful ritual takes place in front of the modern Basilica of Guadalupe, completed in 1977 at Tepeyac at the site of the temple formerly dedicated to Goddess Tonantzin. A group of women and men, attired in costumes inspired by the traditional Aztec ritual garb and carrying musical instruments, appears in a ritual procession in front of the awaiting public that parts to let them through. The procession stops in front of the main entrance to the Basilica, and then the dances, percussion sounds, music and chanting take place. They intone praises to their Heavenly Queen, Coatlicue-Guadalupe-Tonantzín, while the entranced public watches. These people celebrate their Aztec heritage and ties to the Omnipotent Aztec Mother. Mexican people are very proud of their native culture, the great civilization that engendered Guadalupe and her miracles.

I experienced a deeply spiritual state of mind as I witnessed one of these events, together with the crowd of thousands standing on the stone platform, the *zócalo,* of the temple. That day left an indelible impression on me, prompting me to try to comprehend the mystical nature of the Guadalupan religion. At that time I realized that the shape of the basilica was in line with the indigenous thinking: it was circular, and extended like a teepee into the sky. The interior of the Basilica is designed to let the rays of the sun penetrate the glass, bathing the inner space in light; it can accommodate ten thousand people. The architect, Pedro Ramirez Vasquez, was sensible to the public's desire for a spiritual space worthy of a major religious center of the Americas, and he successfully accomplished his goal.

The people of the Americas intuitively respond to the mystical presence of the *tilma,* the new Holy Grail, with sublime devotion. Yet, the Guadalupan presence at Tepeyac, as well as at numerous other locations of the Americas is still obscured by the fact that the church fathers, standing inside their altar spaces, tend to ignore the presence of the Great Mother at her sacred locations by rarely referring to her during their religious functions. Therefore, her spiritual presence and the messages she sends are officially silenced. This is unfortunate, since we should pay attention to these powerful divine manifestations – and they keep occurring. Yet they are often underreported and underutilized, and their potential benefit to humanity is partially lost. Other miraculous sites of the Madonna are even more neglected by the patriarchal establishment; they do not have the support system of the shamanic priestesses of Guadalupe. All the miraculous sites of the Virgin Mary are visited frequently, and the miracle cures are spectacular, but how much more attuned could our spirit become if and when the official support system would work properly and fairly? This we have yet to find out. Meantime, Guadalupan presence is among us. If we want to pay attention, we can help ourselves by reaching out toward her unconditional energy of love. In spite of the official lack of interest in the apparitions of the Madonna, her spiritual influence is of great socio-cultural importance, and is on the increase. The Madonna-Mary-Guadalupe represents the female aspect of the Christian God and is viewed by the avant-garde theologians, particularly by those of Latin heritage, as the divine feminine of Christian doctrine and as the Savior of the oppressed and dispossessed. She is the *mestiza,* and as a mixture of the indigenous and the Hispanic *razas*, represents the Latin folk of the Americas.[5] She, therefore, has huge importance as the validation of the feminine spirituality – the nurturer, the compassionate and loving Great Mother of the Americas, and a powerful sacred energy that emanates from the energy source, the All That Is. Her appeal to Latin women is amazing, but American women of every background are attracted to her mystical, mythical, and archetypal persona. She is the Goddess of the Americas that represents the feminine essence of Mother Earth and female spirituality that is rooted in love, peace, and compassion, and which manifests global life forces within the universal continuum of time and space.

4.

Kyra Belán

2

Lady Liberty: The American Sun Goddess

On a windy and cold day in March my husband and I were on our way to visit the ultimate symbol of the United States of America, the Colossus of the New World, known as the Statue of Liberty. We arrived by subway from upper Manhattan to New York's Battery Park to catch the Circle Line-Statue of Liberty Ferry that would take us to the Liberty Island, a place where the bigger than life symbol for freedom stands overlooking the New York Harbor. After purchasing our tickets we stood in line for nearly thirty minutes, while chilling winds easily penetrated our bodies through the garments. Since the terrorist attack of 2001 on the World Trade Center, known as the tragic *nine-eleven* event, everyone must go trough the security checkpoint before boarding the tour boat, and the option of climbing inside the statue into its colossal head was no longer available at that time, due to the horrific event when the planes hijacked by suicidal terrorists destroyed the Twin Towers and caused irreparable damage, death, and hardship to the people of New York, the nation, and the entire world. This event forever changed our perception of reality, and our awareness of the mythos behind the grand Lady has been sharpened.

The Statue of Liberty is a powerful symbol for the American democracy. This archetypal Goddess, a direct prototype of the ancient Roman Goddess of Liberty, oversees the harbor as she stretches her torch-bearing arm into the skies. This gigantic woman, made out of copper, has acquired through time a green coloring or *patina*. Her newly restored torch glows as the rays of the sun bounce off its golden flames.

Her reassuring presence exerts a calming effect on the visiting public: she is the physical and symbolic embodiment for the principles of democracy in America.

Our tour boat slowly circumnavigated the Liberty Island. Aboard, every passenger, whether an American or a foreign tourist, a child or an adult, was *a priori* familiar with Lady Liberty through media exposure such as television, movies, personal computers, cell phones, books, magazines, and postcards sold all over the city of New York and worldwide. Many had observed her from afar, from the boats that navigated by, or from the planes that flew over the harbor to land at one of the airports nearby. When our ferry approached the island, the colossal statue could be seen from a closer vantage point. The ferry, generating some rippling of the waves, curved around the Goddess, allowing the curious passengers numerous frontal, side, and the less familiar back views. The giant green woman's seven-pronged solar nimbus was slowly morphing, as the rules of perspective gradually distorted its proportions. The spectators, impressed, paraded around the vessel, craned their necks, snapped pictures, shot video, and loudly discussed their impressions of the famous American symbol for freedom.

As soon as the boat arrived on the island, we quickly headed for the café and the adjacent gift shop. Many souvenirs of the statue were sold there, featuring the familiar image printed on mugs, banners, and postcards. I was particularly impressed by the miniature three-dimensional replicas of Lady Liberty executed to scale in a variety of sizes. The reproductions were painted green and held up their golden torches; they were designed to emulate the recently restored version of the Statue of Liberty. We stepped outside, where we could see bundled up groups of tourists who constantly clicked their state of the arts digital cameras, while some were recording the giant statue with their digital camcorders. The wind was harsh and cold, but it did not stop anyone from photographing The Lady. I enthusiastically joined the rest of the visitors, busily shooting my own memories. As I looked at the giant statue through my view finder, I was experiencing a mixture of feelings: reverence, patriotism, spirituality, and love for this mythical woman-archetype: I was in the presence of a sacred icon, similar to the divine Lady of Guadalupe, but instead of the ritual offerings of flowers or candles, the crowd was participating in their private rituals of photographic sessions, capturing forever a particular instance in time: as a personal experience, an image for good luck, a sacred icon, and a unique event. Some families and couples asked other visitors to take their pictures to record these moments for the rest of their lives, so they could show them to their relatives and friends, or to their future children or grandchildren.

There was a genuine feeling of reverence emanating from the public: Lady Liberty deeply affected her pilgrims of the new millennium. The gigantic woman represented an historical heritage embedded in the arts, culture, religions, and myths of our society. Gifted to the American people by the people of France, she has been accessible to the public for visits that included a confining climb inside the architectural statue all the way up into her crown. The public could even climb into her torch; no other statue in the world could offer its entire interior space as well as exterior to her people, a metaphor for a mother's womb. But she may never be as freely accessible to her admiring public as she was before the tragic events of

September eleven of 2001. Yet, as usual, she stands as a powerful symbol for America. As an icon of freedom, she is admired by the entire world.

Lady Liberty is the largest sculpture of a woman in existence; the height of the statue from its base to the tip of the torch is 151 feet and one inch, or 46 meters; or, according to the 1984 survey it is 152 feet and 2 inches or 46.84 meters. However, the height of Liberty with the pedestal, from the bottom of the base to the end of the torch is 305 feet, or 93 meters, or according to the same survey 306 feet and 8 inches, or 93.47 meters. The colossal goddess is made out of 310 riveted copper plates that are approximately 3/32 of an inch thick.[6] She has been measured extensively; for her curious admirers the measurements can be easily found on the internet by typing her name into a search engine, such as Google. The original French name of the Lady is the *Statue of Liberty Enlightening the World*, or *Liberty Illuminating the World*. These official titles reflected the idea of a matriarchal spirituality behind this gift from the French people to the American people. The artwork is the creation of a French sculptor Frederic Auguste Bartoldi (1834-1904). The official inauguration of the completed statue, situated on the Liberty Island, called Bedloe's Island at that time, took place on twenty-eight of October of 1886.[7]

Since then, the popularity of Lady Liberty has multiplied in geometric progression; her symbolic presence as the embodiment for democratic principles is currently at its peak. The Americans love their Lady, and her image is constantly used in advertising, television, the internet, the fine arts, film and video, graphic arts, entertainment, political cartoons, tee shirts, postal stamps, and more. She represents the social values of this country, and she is also an American Goddess. The divine source of inspiration for Bartoldi, as he worked on the preliminary sketches for the commission, was the Goddess of Liberty of ancient Romans, a particularly favorite divinity of the already freed slaves, and the slaves seeking freedom. Lady Liberty's attire is inspired by two garments worn by the goddesses and women of Ancient Rome: the *stola*, a long dress that nearly covers a woman's feet, and the *palla*, or the garment that is worn over the *stola* and fastened over the left shoulder. One of the temples of the Goddess of Liberty was built during second century B C E, and many slaves or freed slaves worshiped her there. This Goddess became more popular in ancient Rome during the fourth century as a consequence of the newly established law of freedom, and her statue was placed in the forum of the great city of Rome.

The new American version of the goddess was promptly accepted and embraced by the enthusiastic public, and it seemed appropriate that, like in ancient Roman times, the statue would have a sacred ceremony: she was blessed by the Protestant ministers at her inaugural ceremony that took place in 1886. In 1937, to commemorate the hundred and fiftieth anniversary of the U.S. Constitution and to honor the presence of the Goddess of Liberty, the Altar of Liberty was set up on the island. It was decorated with a liberty bell and thirteen stars, while a replica of the Lady, about four feet tall, was placed on the altar. Large white candles were lit in her honor. Several American flags surrounded the ceremonial altar. In addition, offerings of flowers from her devoted public were placed at the base of the altar. Since the Statue of Liberty was officially proclaimed to be a beacon in 1877, provisions were made to improve the lighting that emanated from her torch, her body, and the surrounding environment. When the statue had to be restored between 1982 and 1986, the lighting around the statue was improved even more: a powerful stream of light now seems to emanate from her head. This last improvement, together with several other projects designed to further enhance the Lady Liberty's illumination process, was the most successful in increasing her presence during the evening hours.[8]

An extraordinary goddess, the Statue of Liberty does not exclusively derive her identity from the Roman Goddess of Freedom, but has ties to other female divinities, including Mary, the Christian Mother of God. The halo of seven prongs around her head connects her to the numerous Sun Goddesses of Ancient times, including those of Old Europe and Africa. The Sun Goddesses, worshiped all over the globe during the thousands of years of matriarchal cultures and during early patriarchal societies, are the descendants of the Great Mother Goddess of the Paleolithic and Neolithic eras. In Egypt, possibly the oldest known divinity was the Great Goddess Sekhmet, who is represented in sculpture and paintings wearing a solar disc on her lioness faced head; she is also the mother of the male Sun God Ra. The Great Goddess Isis of the Egyptians was also a solar divinity, and both goddesses were often interpreted as aspects of each other. Sekhmet was believed to have awesome powers over life and death, and like the Hindu Goddess Kali, was both the creator and transformer of life. During the beginnings of Egyptian patriarchy Sekhmet became the war goddess. Yet, her qualities as the Goddess of Light and a Sun Goddess equated her with the beloved Goddess Isis.

The religion of the Sun Goddess Isis, predecessor of the solar Lady Liberty, has a long history of existence, more than twice as long as Christianity. This religion spread from Egypt throughout the world of antiquity and eventually posed a threat to the very existence of Christianity. The Egyptians venerated her as the Giver of Life, the Savior, the Redeemer, the Magician, and the Healer. The old Egyptian scriptures state: "In the Beginning there was Isis, Oldest of the Old. She was the *Goddess from Whom all Becoming Arose*. In other words, she was the creator Goddess, and she also gave birth to the Sun, the life giving force of nature. She was celebrated in a Roman variation of her cult as *The One Who is All*. Second century Roman writer Lucius of Patrae, who authored *Metamorphosis*, praises the Goddess in the hymn as the redeemer of human race:

> "O Thou holy and eternal Savior of the human race…Thou bestowest mother's tender affections on the misfortunes of the unhappy mortals… Thou dispellest the storms of life and stretchest forth thy right hand of salvation, by which thou unravellest even the inextricably tangled web of Fate… Thou turnest the Earth in its orb; Thou givest light to the sun: Thou rulest the world; Thou treadest Death underfoot. To Thee the stars are responsive; by Thee the seasons turn and the goddesses/gods rejoice and the elements are in subjection…"[9]

The worshipers of Isis were introduced into her religion through the initiations into the Mysteries of Isis. Each initiate experienced an unforgettable series of rituals and, as a result, many had intense visions of the Great Mother. The Savior Goddess appeared to them as the being of light, and this enlightening experience opened for them the road to salvation, not only in their present lives, but also in the afterlife. Isian texts explained that the Goddess disclosed the mysteries of the stars and could miraculously stop the Sun and slow down the flow of the waters. Isis was also known to produce many other miracles that later inspired the various writers of Christian scriptures. This Savior of humanity was worshiped throughout the world up to the sixth century C E, and at that time she was cleverly absorbed into Christianity as the Christian Mother of God, the Virgin Mary. To the early Christians she was an amalgamation of Mary and Isis, the Savior and Creator Mother of all. Her symbol, the ankh or looped cross, was to become the future symbol of the Christian male God and Christianity in a modified form of a cross.

Sun Goddesses ruled in ancient Europe during the era of matriarchal myths. In fact, the word Sun often denoted female gender, although when patriarchal order took hold, the gender of the Sun was often changed from feminine to masculine, as the new male Sun Gods emerged. In England, the old word for Sun is Sunne, a feminine noun. The Anglo-Saxons named their Sun Goddess Sunna, while the East Anglians called her Phoebe. The rituals performed for the Sun Goddesses were scheduled during the solstices and spring equinox celebrations, and the ritual items included the disc shaped objects and chariots that the mythical Goddesses rode into the sunsets. In Germany, Sweden, Norway and Denmark the word Sun denotes the feminine gender to this day. Sól was the name of the Nordic Sun Goddess who drove her chariot across the sky, while Germans called her Sunna; her husband was the Moon God. Fire and light were also associated with the Sun Goddess, and her healing powers were widely in demand during the rituals. The beliefs related to this Sun Goddess depicted her as also the Goddess of the Underworld, where she retired at night.

The Ancient Romans worshiped their Sun Goddess as Juno Lucina. The Christian church fathers changed her name to saint or Santa Lucia; although diminished, she was still associated with light, luminosity, and the gift of seeing. The Goddess Oestre, considered by the Ancient Saxons to be the daughter of Sól, was celebrated during the spring season with a ritual to honor her abilities to promote abundance in nature. Like other Pagan cultures, the Baltic area populated by Lituanians, Latvians and Prussians, descendants of the Indo-Europeans, worshiped the Sun Goddess Saule. According to the ancient myth this Goddess was also the creator of the world which she formed out of an egg shaped mass.[10] The Virgin Mary was closely associated with these Pagan divinities, and she was worshiped as the Sun Goddess during Christianity up to the renaissance times, although not officially recognized as such by the church fathers, who consistently cast doubts on her divine status.

In the Near East the Hittites populated most of Anatolia, the land of the ancient matriarchal Goddess-worshiping culture. They worshiped a Sun Goddess and her daughter, also a solar divinity, while they venerated numerous other goddesses. Many versions and changes took place in the myths of Ancient Greece when the invading Indo-European tribes were blended with the indigenous and established matriarchal Mycenaeans. During earlier period, Sun Goddess Helia was the original version of the Sun God Helios. Later, she was interpreted as the daughter of the same Sun God just as the omnipotent Goddess Athena became the daughter of Zeus during the patriarchal times of ancient Greece. All andro-centric societies routinely changed older matriarchal myths that featured powerful Goddesses into new versions more suitable for their regime that classified women as less important than men. Solar daughters of Helios, the new male Sun God, were Pasiphae and Circe, well known within the patriarchal versions of Classical Greece. Pasiphae became the wife of Minos, the king of Crete; she gave birth to the Minotaur. Circe was the Queen of

Colchis. Her symbol was the hawk, a bird commonly associated in ancient myths with solar divinities such as Isis.[11]

By association, early versions of Goddess Athena of ancient Greece retained many powers of her former omnipotent self, and still included powers of creation. Her headdress consists of prongs shaped as owls and horses. The owl is symbolic of wisdom, while the horse is strongly associated with omnipotent solar goddesses of ancient and prehistoric times. These "sun rays" are reminiscent of the halo of the statue of Liberty. Her flowing garments are similar as well, and her majestic demeanor as the protector of her people is akin to the posture of power of the American Goddess. Like the Lady Liberty, Athena received much admiration from her worshipers who saw her as their protector. The Savior Goddess Athena granted assurance to the Athenians that their country would stay free.

The most remote ancestor of the Statue of Liberty can be traced to the Paleolithic and Neolithic eras, early times on the planet when God was usually visualized as a woman. Devoted followers carved numerous images of the Great Mother. Many of these sculptures were portable, and were carried around as the nomadic tribes moved from one territory to another. On the contrary, the colossal sculpture of Lady Liberty is highly visible, and extremely familiar to nearly everyone all over the world. She was created at a time when female archetypal images started to emerge from the subconscious minds of the world's population, a process that still continues today. The timeliness of this archetype, her larger than life presence, and her symbolic nature establishes Lady Liberty as a mythical goddess of colossal proportions. The Goddess of Liberty and other ancient Roman divinities are all fractions of the pre-historic Great Mother. Filtered through time, the myths associated with the Great Goddess and her descendants have been inherited by our civilization and are our historical heritage. Some of these myths are examined in the chapters that follow.

The impact of the physical presence of the giant statue at the harbor of New York, perceived as the greatest city on Earth, is felt all over the planet. The message of freedom, power, spirituality, and beauty of American culture is clearly conveyed: the Lady is the symbol that represents a possible future of the worldwide freedom and equality.

Kyra Belán

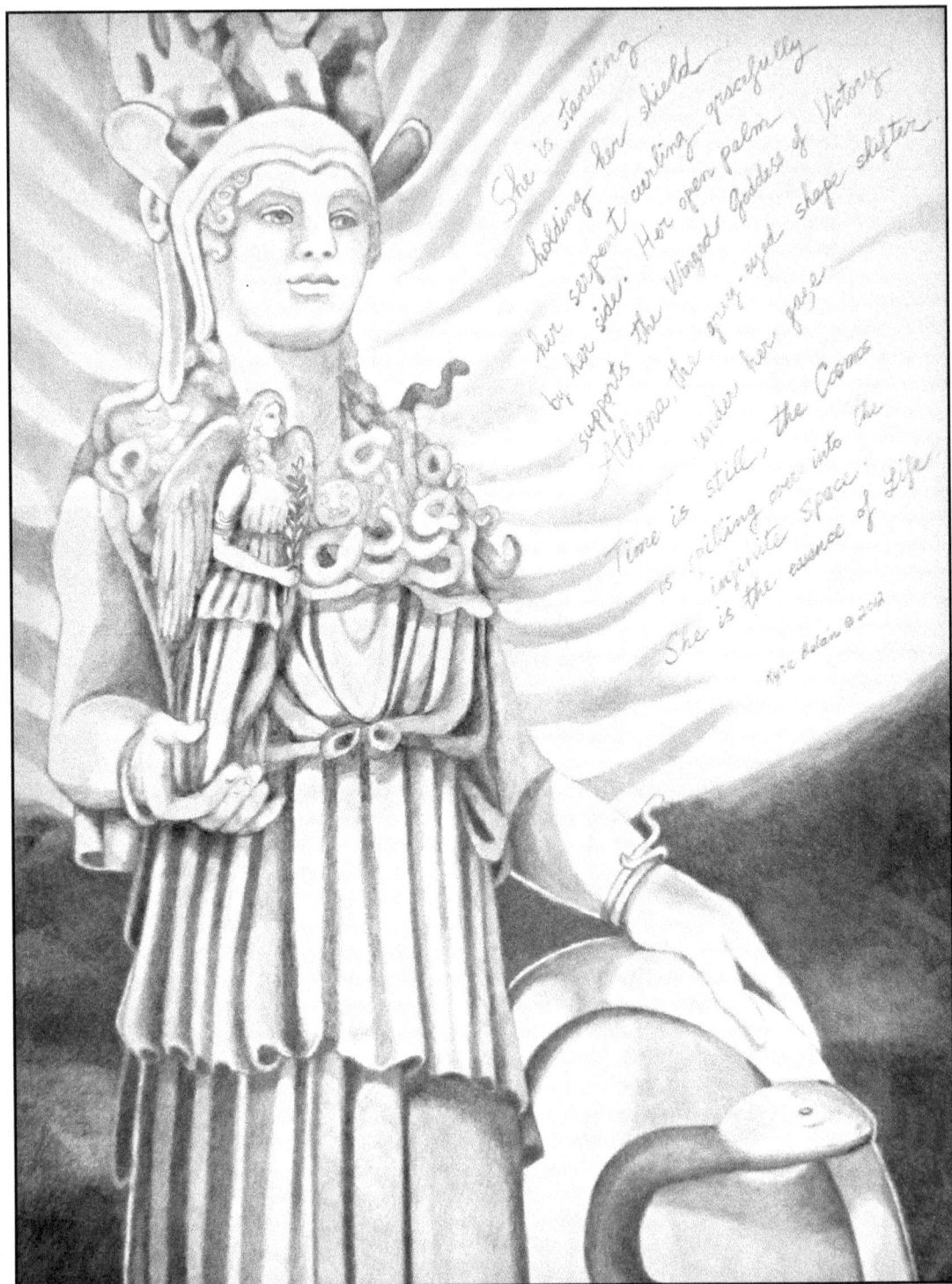

She is standing,
holding her shield,
her serpent curling gracefully
by her side. Her open palm
supports the Winged Goddess of Victory.
Athena, the grey-eyed shape shifter,
under her gaze,
Time is still, the Cosmos
is spilling over into the
infinite space,
She is the essence of Life.

Kyra Belán © 2012

5.

3

Goddess Athena and her American Parthenon

Goddess Athena, one of the ancestors of the archetypal Lady Liberty, has a temple in America that equals in beauty and scale those that were built for her in ancient Greece circa two thousand years ago. Through her we can reconnect to our Ancient Classical heritage of Western civilization. This Goddess is a part of the women's movement, spirituality movement, New Age movement, and the Pagan American movement. She deeply appeals to the mythologists, art historians, artists, art lovers, and cultural historians. Her presence in America has helped many to understand, relate to, and access the heritage of the Old World. Her American temple is a public place and a museum; it also serves as a school for children, and a research center for college students and scholars. The statue of the Goddess is a carefully researched and executed reproduction of the original of the same size that was located in her temple completed circa 438 B C E in Ancient Greece. Radiant, the golden Sun Goddess of America stands within the sanctuary of a full-scale replica of her original temple, the Parthenon. The ruins of the original Parthenon are located on the Acropolis Hill in Athens, Greece, where the temple is the primary tourist attraction. It is regarded as the apex of the ancient Greek's achievement in architecture.

A Temple for the American Athena

The Nashville's Parthenon is a structure to be admired. It was originally completed in 1897 for the Centennial Exposition, and then rebuilt in the nineteen twenties as a full-scale replica, created to emulate the original temple as close as possible. The presence of this building in Nashville, Tennessee established the city as a culturally significant and sophisticated *Athens of the South*. The statue of the Goddess, however, was added sixty years later during the early eighties, when the need for Athena's image became apparent. A temple without its principal inhabitant is incomplete, and this correction had to be made at a time when, due to the women's movement, serious research was launched in all areas of sciences, humanities, and the arts, rewriting the facts from a more inclusive perspective in order to integrate the accomplishments of women and female mythologies into the mainstream culture. The inclusion of women into the social discourse sparked new interest in the recovery of female archetypes, symbols, myths, and legends. Goddess Athena, who had endured as such for millennia, became a part of this new research, thus making her physical presence at her American temple a necessity. The commission to create the sculpture was awarded to Alan LeQuire, an artist from Nashville. He learned about the historical background of the statue, helped by the information gathered by several noted scholars of the classical Greek art. LeQuire based his visual image on this research, a difficult task since the original statue that stood inside the Greek Parthenon, completed by Pheidias and dedicated around 437 B C E, was lost and is believed to be destroyed.

Athena Parthenos of Nashville stands forty-one feet and ten inches high, the same size as the original. According to the best available sources she is the largest indoor statue in America and the world. In her right hand she holds six feet tall Nike, the Goddess of Victory, and an aspect of herself. Her left hand is resting on her shield, with her magical serpent coiled inside. The statue was made of gypsum cement in many sections by LeQuire in his studio, and then assembled inside the Parthenon. In 2002 it became apparent that the whiteness of the Nashville Athena did not measure up to the stunning beauty of the gold covered original, and the artist, together with the gilder Lou Reed, was commissioned to guild the statue, so the colossal replica would look closer to the Greek original. Athena was gilded in 23.75 Karat Italian gold, which covers her long garment, her headdress, her shield, the entire statue of Nike, and the serpent coiled inside the shield. The gold leaf was originally delivered in little booklets of twenty-five sheets measuring approximately three square inches each. Before it was applied to the sculpture, three coats of shellac and a coat of sizing were brushed on to cover the surface. The sizing was the glue medium to which the gold was attached. The last process consisted of the application of gold leaf squares and the brushing off of any excess gold. To smooth out the overlapping seams, the statue of Athena was gently rubbed down with ice water and cotton, which completed the process. Her skin was painted to simulate both the ancient ivory tones of the original statue and the natural look of human skin. This complex process took less than four months, and the statue today radiates golden hues and dazzles the visitors in a manner similar to the ancient Goddess that captivated and mesmerized the worshipers nearly two and a half thousand years ago.

The Myth of Athena

Athena has a complex mythological background. Originally an omnipotent Mother-Creator of prehistoric matriarchal times, and later the omnipotent Goddess that was worshiped by a matriarchal civilization that flourished on the island of Crete, she ruled over both of these peaceful civilizations. Then, as the patriarchal invaders from northeast brought the male War God with them and conquered ancient Greece, Athena was transformed by the newer myth into the daughter of Zeus and Goddess of War. She, however, retained many of her original powers; she was the protector and supreme Goddess of the Athenians, also the Goddess of wisdom, of the arts, and the Weaver of Destinies. Her people adored her, and her temples were numerous, monumental, and exquisite. The Parthenon was the perfect Doric temple, the largest built in Greece, and it contained her original colossal statue. The city of Athens was named after her, and she was evoked during the times of danger for protection and for enduring times of peace. During the era of Classical Greece, Athena's myth was modified to suit an increasingly patriarchal society: her father Zeus became her sole parent, and she pledged allegiance to him alone. Yet the vestiges of her original myth remained, and she continued to wear the symbols of matriarchy. Athena's *aegis* displays a depiction of the snake haired head of Medusa, a goddess known as the protector and an aspect of Athena herself; and the serpent under her shield is symbolic of the Earth Mother. In the new millennium, matriarchal myths about Athena are being re-discovered and re-learned; consequently a more complete image of the Goddess is emerging. In contemporary times the original matriarchal versions of the myths have become relevant: they mirror our peace-starved society better than many outdated patriarchal myths. People are attracted to the matriarchal myths and legends, as they have much to offer to the post-modern minds. Today Athena is the mythical goddess that has a sacred place within human psyche.

Two distinct versions of Athenian myths co-exist to explain the Goddess: one that was accepted during the patriarchal times, and a more current one that stems from the original matriarchal roots. The latter explains the Goddess as the triple goddess: the Creator (The Virgin), the Nurturer (The Mother) and the Wise Protector (The Crone). This last aspect is also Medusa, who was originally the Mother-Protector. It is likely that Athena was the same omnipotent Great Goddess that the matriarchal Crete worshiped throughout the antiquity for thousands of years. However, the patriarchal myth transformed her into the daughter of the dominant male God. According to this myth, Zeus swallowed Athena's pregnant mother Metis, the Earth Goddess, thus appropriating the roles of both the father and the mother. This unusual process established him as a male capable of giving birth, ability natural only to a woman. Thus, by becoming her sole parent, Zeus hoped to have Athena's love, allegiance, and support entirely for himself. The new myth was engendered during the religious-philosophical climate in ancient Greece that contributed to the deterioration of the rights of women. Accordingly, the new patriarchal Athena became the enemy of Medusa, and transformed her into the snake headed monster.

In spite of all the anti-female aspects of this patriarchal myth, many contemporary women appreciate and celebrate this Goddess. Athena is the archetype appreciated by women who seek strength, self-confidence, leadership abilities, and creativity. She represents the inner goddess for those women who are leaders living in a patriarchal society in transition, a role model for women who are the ground-breakers within the male dominated society. Equally important to women is the fact that Athena represents divine wisdom and creativity. Women who are exploring their entelechy as scientists, inventors, theorists, theologians, philosophers, sociologists, and other pioneers within their fields identify with this goddess. For the women who lead, create artworks, discover, and change the face of the world, the Athenian archetype helps legitimize their powers, creativity, and intelligence.

It is safe to conclude that Athena was extremely important to the ancient people of Athens. She was worshiped with fervor, and the best temples of Classical Greece were dedicated to this goddess. The ancient Greek people had never forgotten the peaceful matriarchal times when they worshiped their Great Goddess as their Mother-Creator. Even during the most militant patriarchal times, men and women loved and worshiped their original omnipotent Goddess Gaia, who was considered the primordial Mother of All Creation, and the Mother of all the goddesses and gods. She was the *primary one*, the ultimate beginning. It was not surprising that the militant patriarchal Greece transformed their creator Mother Goddess of Wisdom and the Arts into the Goddess of War; Athena was needed in that capacity to give the militant Greeks courage to wage their frequent wars. Yet she was still the divinity of great powers, luminous and quasi-omnipotent. Her popularity in the region of Athens exceeded that of other gods and goddesses, including Zeus. Her main temple, the Parthenon, not only was a sacred place, together with the rest of the temples of the famous Acropolis, but historical research points out that it also was the location that contained most of the country's treasures, including the solid gold garments that adorned her original giant statue. Goddess Athena has much to offer to people today; women see themselves in her, as they navigate through the complex, dangerous, and busy world, while the men see their wives, daughters and mothers mirrored in her. Ultimately, she is also the nurturing Earth Mother, giving us not only the gift of the olive tree, but also the gift of all the resources of nature.

Nashville's Parthenon is located in the Centennial Park. A side view of the structure was clearly visible on a low grassy hill as my husband and I approached the temple from the highway, and our car turned into the entrance of this park. The sunlit warm tones of the temple were contrasting against the cool blue of the sky. As we approached the building, a lake also became visible. A colorful sculpture of a catfish, one of the many that were seen around the city of Nashville as a result of a local Art in Public Places program, was located in front of the lake. Small groups of tourists and visitors were scattered around the lake among the lush green carpet of grass bathed by the sun. The Doric temple, an exact replica of the original in terms of architectural proportions and details, was not made out of marble like the temple that stands on the Acropolis Hill in Athens, Greece; it was instead built out of concrete[12] and its color was yellowish tan, rather than white. The surfaces of the building were treated with a mixture of gravel, cement and crushed ceramic tile to achieve a textural and warm toned surface. The relief sculptures of the pediments, researched reproductions, had painted backgrounds like those of the original Greek temple during its days of the Classical era, before the damage due to the passage of time took place. We parked the car in a conveniently located lot and headed for the temple, anticipating a unique and memorable experience.

The current entrance to the temple was added below the platform of the structure by interrupting the steps that led to the original entrance. It takes the visitors into the lobby, the gift shop, and the art galleries that display both the permanent and the visiting collections. To enter the *cella* of the temple, one must walk up the steps to the next level, and then through the monumental bronze doors worthy of the Parthenon built by the ancient Greeks. Upon entering, I was immediately faced with the giant statue of Athena, in glittering gold, located at the opposite end of the *naos*. The nearly forty-two foot high Goddess was wearing her five-prong headdress with the sphinx in the center, two horses on each side, and the two flaps of the helmet standing up to signify that she was at peace. The golden goddess was holding the six foot high statue of Nike, the Goddess of Victory, in her right hand, while her spear and her large round shield were located to her left. Her left hand was resting on the shield that held the coils of her sacred serpent. Her head, high above the crowd, could only be seen from a low vantage point, yet her large blue-grey eyes stood out beneath the golden lashes, and her full lips were painted red; these colors softened her classical features, perhaps making the Goddess more accessible as a feminine archetype of divine wisdom, creativity, and protection.

Entranced by the glimmer of the golden Goddess, I was trying to etch in my mind every detail of the spectacular vision. The gold surfaces of her *aegis*, fringed by the serpents and with the head of Medusa in the center; and her *peplos* dress, with the folds gracefully cascading toward the platform and partly covering her sandals, were similar to the dazzling garments contemplated by the worshipers of ancient Athens that looked at the Goddess as she stood inside the original Parthenon. The golden helmet proclaimed her as the descendant of the omnipotent Mother God of the matriarchal past, also a Sun Goddess. Athena certainly was the supreme God of the Athenians, and their Savior, like Isis or the Virgin Mary in her occult form, when celebrated during the times of medieval Christianity in Europe. The ambiance of the *naos*, dwarfed by the size of its sacred inhabitant, was solemn. The magnificent environment replicated in me the emotions that I felt when I visited the original Parthenon on the Acropolis Hill in Greece, and visualized what Athena would look like, a colossal figure standing inside her temple in front of a reflective pool of water. I felt grateful to the many people who made this recreation of Athena and the Parthenon possible in Nashville, appropriately called the Athens of the South.

In ancient times, Athena was depicted in her myths as the mentor of her people, the magnificent *shape shifter* who appeared to her devotees at the time of need in various forms, female and male. Her apparitions were not always instantly recognizable, as she often preferred to help incognito. In contemporary life, Athena's archetype changes people in many positive and constructive ways: wisdom, power, and creativity are all within her realm of gifts she can award to humankind. Today the Goddess represents Nashville, Tennessee as the spirit of the American South and of America.

To trace the ancestry of the grey-eyed goddess, we must retreat deep into the prehistory of thousands of years ago. During those matriarchal times, women were respected as creators. The Great Goddess, triple in nature, ruled their world, including the territory that later became Greece. She was the primordial Gaia from which the Earth, and all the divinities were born. According to the myth generated during the patriarchal times, a second generation of the divinities was born of her, and they were called the Titans. Later Rhea and Cronos, two of the divine Titans, gave birth to the group of goddesses and gods that were called the Olympians by the ancient Greeks. The newly formed patriarchal pantheon of classical Greece had divided the powers of the Great Goddess into a number of goddesses and gods. Still, the goddesses were powerful, and therefore their myths are relevant today. To American women that are consciously searching for their personal archetypes and myths, several of these goddesses are so inspirational that they rival the greatest myths of Athena. I will briefly cover a few of the myths, starting with the primordial Gaia.

The Mythical Gaia: The Origin of the Universe

Gaia is the original parthenogenic Goddess of the ancient Greece. She is the initial Creator of all: the cosmos, the sky, the earth, and the underworld. She operates through life and death. She is the universe, the whole of time, the eternity; she has no beginning and no end. She is all that is and will be. Everything came from Gaia, including the female and the male, the light and the darkness, the animals, the plants and the planet Earth. Even during the zenith of the patriarchal times when in ancient Greece the myths were about the struggle of the female and male and the subsequent subjugation of the female by the male, Gaia never lost her completeness, and was worshiped in her full glory. When she acquired a husband, Uranus, he was subdued by his intense desire for the union with her. A later myth tells us of the children of Gaia and Uranus, a couple called Rhea and Cronos; this couple engendered the well-known Olympian divinities, which include many female and male fractions of Gaia.

The Mysteries of Demeter

The most complex, mystical and archetypal Goddess that belonged to the Olympian group of divinities is the powerful Demeter, the Earth Mother. She, under patriarchy, managed to preserve most of the properties of the complete Great Goddess within herself. Her religious rites were complex, emotional, transformational, and lasted for many days. They included processional pilgrimages, dramatic re-enactments of religious myths, and rituals that were shrouded in secrecy and were never revealed to the world by the initiates. The rituals dedicated to the worship of Demeter are called the Eleusinian Mysteries. They are named after the site of her most important temple at Eleusis, located within a short distance from the city of Athens. Demeter functioned as the Creator Goddess, the Earth Goddess, and the Goddess of Agriculture. Together with her daughter Persephone (also called Kore or Core) and Hecate, the All-knowing Goddess, she formed the female divine Trinity. The

Eleusinian Mysteries, a series of secret rituals, were practiced in ancient Greece for about three thousand years. Each September and October, the people of Greece, headed by the priestesses and priests of Demeter, led a nine day long event, a procession that ultimately arrived at Eleusis where the secret rituals took place. Only the initiates were allowed to go through the re-enactments of the sacred mysteries. Emotionally charged, the rituals transformed the initiates by stimulating their spiritual evolution. Like the participants of the old matriarchal Goddess-worshiping cultures, the initiates were there to achieve their spiritual and personal growth; these initiations were not sacrificial or war related. Since the participants never disclosed the entire activity after they resumed their routine lives, the secret rituals that took place at Eleusis remain partially unknown; therefore, the entire ceremony was never fully recorded in any texts. *The Homeric Hymns*, an anonymous ancient source that may have been written by a woman or several people, gives only a partial description of the sacred events.

It is clear that the Eleusinian Mysteries belong to our matriarchal heritage; they supported the feminine perspective and values that operated within a patriarchal culture of ancient Greece that favored aggression and subjugation. The presence of the Mysteries filled the needs of the people by balancing the dominant patriarchal values with female concerns, such as compassion, cooperation, nurture, and partnership. This religion allowed both genders to explore and nurture their caring and spiritual aspects. Women had the opportunity to be empowered within their roles, and to bond with their female offspring, while experiencing female-based spirituality that placed them on an equal level with men. Thus, the spiritual gifts of Demeter included that of the motherly love, the deep bond between a mother and a daughter, or a mother and a son. The initiation rituals were also about universal love, wellbeing, abundance, and the fulfillment of desires, as Demeter was believed to bestow many gifts upon her worshipers, including plentiful crops, peaceful times, and harmony among the people.

The sacred ruins of the temple at Eleusis are located in the most fertile agricultural area of the land, a fact that corroborates Demeter's role as the Earth Mother and Grain Goddess. According to the Hellenic tradition, the Mother and Daughter Goddesses have been worshiped on that location since *time immemorial*, or around three thousand years, and from that site their worship spread throughout the rest of the land. But another tradition placed Demeter and Kore's origins onto the Island of Crete. However, another indicates that her origins may be further away in Egypt. The similarities between Demeter and the Mother God of the matriarchal Crete are stunning; but many of the Great Goddesses of Egypt, particularly Goddess Isis, also carry similarities to Demeter, as all have descended from the Great Mother worshiped in pre-dynastic Egypt and the old world during prehistory.

The myth of Demeter and Kore contains an archetypal story, embedded with the symbolism of life, death, and resurrection. It is a story about the cycles of nature, revered and explained within the myth through the legend of these Mother and Daughter Goddesses. This myth is the most beautiful and spiritually uplifting story that reached us from the times of ancient Greece, and it is a part of our heritage. It is timeless, and many American women find the legend helpful: it facilitates the re-discovery of the goddess within, and the acceptance of one's creative self. Perhaps the most important aspect of the myth of Demeter and Kore lies in the path of spiritual transformation that it offers. Even though the myth is not completely known, the gaps can be filled in through research, educated guessing, and creative imagination. The power of the ritual activity, as a path toward the positive transformation of human psyche and the affirmation of the benevolent feminine values creates a positive effect on both genders, and may lead humanity toward a constructive and balanced social change.

The myth of Demeter is featured in the ancient *Homeric Hymns*. The story describes her beautiful young daughter Persephone, also known as Kore, playing with the daughters of Oceanus in an idyllic sun drenched meadow covered by an abundance of beautiful flowers. Kore noticed a stunning narcissus flower, and approached it when suddenly the earth opened up, and the God of the Underworld, known as Hades or Pluto, emerged and took her with him; the myth starts as an abduction and a rape story, not uncommon within the myths of patriarchal societies and is an indicator of the times. Hades later served as a prototype for the Devil of Christianity, his underworld becoming the realm of hell. According to the legend, his brother Zeus, the dominant male god of patriarchal Greece, helped Hades the kidnapper/rapist. Hecate, the all-knowing Goddess heard the soul-wrenching cries of Kore/Persephone; however, since she lost some of her powers during the patriarchal times, she could not stop this incident. When Demeter realized that her beloved daughter was gone, she was distraught with grief. She disguised herself as an old woman and roamed the land, desperate. She eventually arrived to the site located near the palace of King Celeus and Queen Metaneira, and sat, grieving, by the well where women usually drew water. There she met the royal couple's beautiful daughters who invited her into the palace; they sensed that there was something extraordinary about the woman. The queen offered her the job of raising her youngest child, the only son. Demeter, treated well by the loving family, took a liking to them, but particularly to the boy, and decided to make him immortal. In order to achieve this she had to dip him into the flames of a fire. The queen, however, spied on her and got upset at seeing what was happening, so the Goddess stopped the process by letting go of the child, who was then picked up by his sisters. Demeter then appeared to everyone as the luminous, golden haired, divine woman of incredible beauty, a Sun Goddess emanating rays of light. Everyone was enchanted by her presence. When she requested that a temple in her honor be erected on the site nearby, the royal couple obeyed, and the king supervised the construction. Within a year the temple was built and was named Eleusis. Demeter entered it and stayed there, grieving for her daughter, while everything on earth started to die. As the Earth Mother, she could take away the abundance and fertility of the earth forever. At that time Zeus, who helped his brother Hades to abduct Kore, ordered him to return her to Demeter; the shifty Hades, however, tricked Kore into eating the fruit called pomegranate, and because of that she was obligated to stay in the underworld six months of each year. The rest of the time she spent with her mother, Demeter. The powerful Earth Goddess, happy to have her daughter back, returned the gifts of fertility and abundance to the formerly richest area of Greece, and the people rejoiced; they could enjoy their life again. Thus, Persephone/Kore initiated her cycle as the Death and Resurrection Goddess. When she emerged from the underworld each spring, nature revived, and when she returned there in autumn and stayed for the winter, nature lay dormant. Demeter, the Salvific Goddess, whose presence at her favorite site, rather than on Olympus with the rest of the divinities, benefited people the most, became the subject of complex, uplifting, and transformative rituals, called the Eleusinian Mysteries. Subsequently, several legends about male divinities that died and were resurrected appeared, including the best-known one, the Christian legend about Jesus.

The Eleusinian Mysteries: What We Know about the Ritual Drama and Reenactment

The Eleusinian Mysteries were enacted as far back as 1350 B C E, according to the inscription on the Parian Marble.[13] The initiations were at first available only to royalty, but eventually everyone - women, men, children, and slaves were admitted. Later even the Roman citizens were given the honor. The only prerequisite to join this religion was that the participants had never killed anyone. There were two parts to the initiations: the first part was the preliminary initiation into the Lesser Mysteries which was held every year in February at the Temple of Demeter and Kore at Agra. The second part was the Greater Mysteries that was held every year for nine days, starting on September fourteen. These rituals took place at Eleusis during the festival, and special envoys were sent out to announce the start of the ceremonies, "to decree that all warring was to cease for two months."[14] The celebratory ritual procession would travel from Eleusis to Athens, headed by the priestesses with the lead priestess carrying the Sacred Chest. The priestesses of Demeter were followed by the entourage, which consisted of the priests, the city authorities, and the numerous faithful. Since every Greek person belonged to the secret religion, they were in the thousands. When it reached the Sacred Lake, several young men met the procession. The men were specially appointed to guard the lake and keep the crowd in order. They initially wore black, but during Roman times the color of their garments was changed to white, the same color as the garments of the initiates. During the procession, flowers and fruit were placed onto the Sacred Road; at this time it was a custom for the worshipers to ask Demeter for healing miracles. As the walk continued, the numbers of people increased. According to ancient documents, as many as 30,000 people would participate in the ritual walks. The faithful rested in Athens, and then followed the Sacred Way to Eleusinion, located below the Propylaea of the Acropolis in the city of Athens. At that time, the lowest ranking priest of the Eleusis came to the Acropolis and announced to the High Priestess of Athena the Protector (*Polyochus*) that Goddess Demeter had arrived to her city. As the procession gathered in the Agora, the Hierophant or High Priest announced the official beginning of the festival and the initiates, dressed in pure white and standing together in a group, received the blessings of the Goddess Demeter. The next day the initiates went to the sea holding young pigs, which they washed and then sacrificed to the Goddess. Their belief was that the pig was the purest animal, and therefore symbolic of the Goddess, and that the sacrificial blood of the animal would cleanse all the hatred and evil out of the soul of the initiate. Also, the pig was the finest gift they could give to their Goddess. Then, they ceremoniously buried the pigs deep into the earth. The next day was spent in Eleusinion, when the initiates offered ritual prayers. The following day special prayers were directed at God Asclepius; according to the tradition he joined the celebration late, but since he was a divinity he was allowed to continue with his initiation. On the last day the procession returned to Eleusis. This was the time of particular joy, as everyone wore wreaths on their heads, carried branches, and stopped to celebrate at every sanctuary on the way. As the nighttime fell, the joyous procession, with their torches in hand, stopped in front of the sanctuary and the initiates were teased for some time, while the priestesses and priests entered the sanctuary immediately. The young women performed a beautiful dance for the people at the sacred well. The next two days, twenty and twenty-one, were the most important to the initiates. Everyone ate the sacred bread, the *pelanos*, made of wheat in honor of Demeter and drank a special drink, called *kikeon*. After this ceremony, they entered the Telesterion for the *telete*, the secret ceremony. There is no record of what took place inside, but a conclusion can be made that a dramatic reenactment of the myth of Demeter took place, during which the initiates symbolically visited the underworld as Persephone did, and emerged back reborn, cleansed, and renewed, into the light of the Great Mother Demeter, in which they rejoiced. Their transformational experience was then completed for the duration of that year.

The rituals that are inspired by the Eleusinian Mysteries, the ancient Greek religion with deep matriarchal roots, are often reenacted in America. Women initiates who are interested in recovering and healing their spirituality that was damaged by the patriarchy usually perform these rituals in small groups. At other times the rituals are re-enacted by mixed gender groups of Neo-Pagans – the women and men interested in discovering and recovering their matriarchal connections as well as their eco-spirituality. These rituals are often re-enacted outdoors within the beauty of nature to celebrate the sacredness of Gaia, our Earth. Goddesses Demeter and Athena are components of the Great Mother, and can be worshiped, admired, or emulated as various aspects of the original omnipotent divinity, the primordial Gaia. Even within the patriarchal Greece, the sacred feminine mythologies endured and remained rich and extensive, offering the people, particularly women, awesome archetypes to choose from as their spiritual role models. Goddess Athena, with whose myths the public is familiar, is a part of our historical heritage that offers us numerous mythical females of ancient Greece.

In the new millennium, Athena is perceived not only as the Goddess of Wisdom, the Arts, and Victory, but also as an aspect of the Great Mother of Old Europe. In a legendary sense she, as the Goddess of America, can be also associated with the mythical Mother Earth of the Native Americans. Athena, ultimately, is an archetypal image of a divine creator in female form. As a shape shifter, she can be whatever we want her to be at different times in our lives. The universality of Athena's mythology allows the Americans people, particularly the millennial generation, to enjoy her in a multitude of ways, fulfilling their particular needs.

6.

Kyra Belán

4

Isis: Egypt in America

The Great Goddess Isis of ancient Egypt has been of particular interest to the Americans since their love affair with ancient Egypt brought her myths and her image into this country during the nineteenth century, and again at the beginning of the twentieth century, when the famous tomb of King Tutankhamen was discovered in 1922. Today the Goddess can be found in the collections of major art museums as a priceless art object, while more recent renditions of Isis can be observed in public places, private homes, businesses, Wiccan and Pagan events, film, video, numerous web sites, and on social media. Most of all, she is in the hearts of the American women as their goddess within, a powerful archetype. Her ancient followers celebrated Isis as the Goddess of Ten Thousand Names. Known as the Great Healer and Magician in the ancient world, her appeal to all the races within the American population corroborates her eternal love affair with the people of this planet. There is a genuine ancient temple – rather a section of one, dedicated to Isis/Hathor - located in New York inside the Metropolitan Museum of Art; it is visited by thousands of tourists, many of whom are there because they wish to be closer to her original place of worship but cannot afford a trip to Egypt. But Americans also travel to Egypt and to many locations in Europe in order to visit her temples and sacred sites, and to spend time there following her myths, seeking her energy, meditating, or worshiping Isis. Yet others visit the Clonegal Castle in Ireland where a contemporary Fellowship of Isis is located; it is a philosophical/religious order that has many adepts and chapters in America and all over the world. Any person can become a member of the Fellowship by applying on the internet and receiving a certificate immediately via their personal computer. There are local chapters in America that follow contemporary versions of this ancient religion, as interpreted and guided by the Fellowship.

Isis is one of the most powerful, magical, mystical, compassionate, and beloved feminine archetypes in America and worldwide. Her ancient religion existed for about four thousand years; it most likely evolved from the Great Goddess worship of the pre-dynastic Egypt. It dominated Egypt and the ancient world throughout the duration of that great culture, and continued into the sixth century. Then it went underground to avoid persecution by the newly formed Christianity. The authorities connected to the early Christian cult forcibly closed her last public temple at Philae in Egypt. She, however, never fully disappeared even under the severest of patriarchal times; she transformed herself, reappearing in a more acceptable form within the new male centered religion as the Virgin Mary, the compassionate Mother of the Christian God. In that form she ruled over Europe and other continents of the world for nearly two thousand years, and upon her arrival in America she became the patron of the new world. She is now recognized   in her true incarnation as the Great Isis, *Oldest of the Old from whom all the beginnings arose* and the eternal *Savior of the human race* to quote the ancient words written by the Roman Apuleius during the 2nd century C E.

As a child growing up in Mar del Plata, a beautiful city in Argentina, I discovered images of Goddess Isis at a library on the pages of books about ancient Egypt, and instantly liked her. To me, she seemed to be an ideal personification of a female face of God: a powerful and dynamic creative force, loving and compassionate. Later, while a student at Arizona State University and in graduate school at Florida State University, I learned about her many temples and rituals and her powers of healing and magic while taking art history classes.

According to her mythology, Isis, in her role as the Great Magician, radiates infinite benevolent energy as she heals and rewards those who ask for her help; her divine love is the purest expression of the ultimate joy of life. The idea that this Goddess is perceived as connected to magic may be the principal reason why people in America are initially attracted to her; if they are interested in healing, Isis is their Goddess. Passionate about life, the Goddess can help us see human existence as a magical process. The emergence of Isis in America seems to be strongly connected to the re-emergence of the Marian apparitions that are frequently taking place in the Americas, and also worldwide. The two female archetypes, nurturing and loving, seem to be merging again in the psyche of people as they did in the past, completing full circle of the mystical voyage of the divine feminine across thousands of years, lands, and waters.

The origins of Isis can be traced to the prehistoric and pre-dynastic Egypt, when thousands of years ago the Great Mother ruled the lands during the Paleolithic and Neolithic times. Goddess Isis exhibits similarities to the prehistoric Bird Goddess, the sky aspect of the Great Mother, having a pair of large and powerful wings. During the dynastic times the Great Goddess was revered in Egypt as several closely related variations such as Sekhmet, Hathor, Bast, and numerous others. The names, the myths and the rituals varied according to the particular geographical regions that celebrated them. To the Ancient Egyptian followers, Isis was always the Great One and ultimately contained within herself all the divinities, female and male. All the goddesses and gods, they believed, were manifestations of Isis, as she encompassed in herself the beginnings of the universe, and the process of creation. Parallel Isian mythology, perhaps more appealing to today's minds developed within a sexist society, was developed by the patriarchal Egypt. According to this myth, the primordial Goddess Nun produced a complete being, Atum, who engendered a couple, the Sky Goddess and the Earth God who were the divine parents of Isis and her brother Osiris. The sister and brother fell in love and engendered Horus: the family then formed a mixed gender Trinity. Isis was central to this myth, as she became the Savior of her brother-husband Osiris, whom she resurrected. The malevolent Seth, their brother, killed the god. Nephtys, another sibling and sister of Isis, was the Queen of the Underworld; she was married to Seth, and can be interpreted as the chthonic aspect of Isis. Isis saved Osiris by finding the pieces of his body that Seth scattered all over Egypt. Piece by piece, Isis put the body of Osiris together and discovered that the *phallus* was still missing. She fashioned one out of clay (or gold, according to another variation of the legend) and helped Osiris perform copulation with her in order to conceive Horus, their son. According to another myth she tricked Sun God Ra, the child of the solar Goddess Sekhmet (who was also an aspect of Isis and Hathor), into passing to her his power to create magic; she thus became the supreme magician and healer of the lands. Miraculous events, such as the parting of the waters (later appropriated for Biblical purposes and found in the Old Testament) and stopping of the Sun (an act of power eventually appropriated by the New Testament), as well as healings performed by Isis (later Jesus did the same in the New Testament), made her the Savior-Healer-Mother Goddess of Egypt. The religion of Isis was adopted by virtually the entire ancient world that stretched from Africa to the Near East, and through Europe as far as England. It remained the most popular cult till Christianity adopted Mary, formerly the Goddess of the Waters.

The tree was an important symbol for the creative aspect of Isis (in one of the myths she extracts Osiris hidden inside a tree); later Christianity adopted it as its own symbol, to be used for the rituals during Christmas holidays. The tree, particularly the sycamore, represented the living, growing and creative energy of Isis. The various rituals dedicated to Isis allowed equal roles for her priestesses and priests. The initiates were expected to participate in the rituals to improve their spirituality. Many rituals have survived, as various occult societies kept the religion of Isis alive through the nearly twenty centuries of Christian oppression. Other rituals, dedicated to the Goddess, were modified and adapted for the Christian church. Currently, rituals of Isis have been revived and recorded by those interested in Neo-Pagan or Wiccan traditions, or those who belong to the world wide Fellowship of Isis. The Goddess is honored by many Americans; she is revered in her old temples in Egypt and within her other ancient sites, in her new houses of worship, at many private or public locations, or with only nature as a backdrop. Many who are seeking to discover their spirituality and their Goddess within are attracted to the rituals developed by the religion of Isis through thousands of years of spiritual practices.

Like all the other religious traditions of the world, the mythologies of Isis, due to the huge span of time of their existence, have undergone many changes. These groups of myths were not in accord with each other even in ancient times, and allowed for variations in the myths. This was particularly apparent in the versions of the myths that explain the Goddess during later stages of Egyptian patriarchy; the newer myths were always less favorable to the divine feminine, since the male priesthood gradually diminished the importance of the divine feminine within their traditions. The public, however, was happy with the older versions, and all these myths co-existed simultaneously. It did not seem to bother the ancient Egyptians that their beloved Isis had several legends; she was still their Universal Creator, the First One, the Mother of all the Goddesses and Gods. At the same time she was one of the divine children of the Sky goddess Nuit or Nut and the Earth God Geb. According to the latest version of the myth, Nut and Geb belonged to the third generation of gods, while Isis was a part of the fourth.

Isis, the reincarnation of the much older prehistoric Bird Goddess/Sky Goddess and the Snake Goddess/Earth Mother, was also the Sacred Sky Cow. The Sun, the Moon, and the stars Sothis and Sirius were symbolic of Isis. She can be interpreted as an aspect of Hathor who also had a son named Horus - they are really one and the same; Isis is also Sekhmet, the lioness-headed Sun Goddess, and Bast the Cat Goddess. It seemed logical that the Egyptians, believers in reincarnation, were certain that their Goddess often re-visited them adopting various physical forms, including that of the actual bird of prey. As the Goddess on Earth, in her role of a Savior, she was seen as loving and caring, and that may be the secret of her long lasting popularity across the planet.

In her role as the Star of Sirius, together with her solar and lunar powers, Isis controlled what the Egyptians believed as the origin of all life – water, including the water of the river Nile. She, therefore, was celebrated in the rituals that took place near and around this river, and, as her religion expanded through the ancient world, near the shores of the seas and rivers elsewhere. Many of these traditions were preserved and were re-enacted when she was later celebrated as Mary the Mother of God, and are still practiced in many European countries. Isis, as the Goddess of Nature, ruled over the seasons, but she also had an access to the spiritual realm, and her powers of resurrection were unsurpassed by any Goddess or God from the mythologies of Ancient Egypt.

Throughout the territories of the ancient world, which included Egypt, Near East and Europe, Isis has been called the Goddess of Ten Thousand Names, or *Isis Mirionymos*, and for four thousand years, she, as the Great Mother, was the answer to the religious needs of humanity; in pre-Christian times the world adored its Mother, and for them she represented the universal divine essence. As the Mother of all the Goddesses and Gods, Isis possessed the supreme power and owned the hearts of the Egyptian people. Her various myths, not necessarily consistent with each other, are usually found in the *Book of the Dead*, the *Book of Coming Forth*, and the *Pyramid Texts* (the writings on the walls of the pyramids and temples). She had accumulated, since her origins as the Primordial Goddess of Creation, such names as the Divine Mother, Lady of Magic, Goddess of Nature, Patroness of Women, Lady of Sacred Sexuality, Goddess of the Mysteries, Mistress of Hermetic Wisdom, the Giver of Life, the Goddess of Myriad Names, and the Mother of the Gods.[16] The universality of this Goddess of Ten Thousand Names can be better understood by examining the many interconnections between her and other Egyptian divinities. The ancient

Egyptians saw Isis as the Creator who assumed many divine personas, some of which will be examined in this chapter.

Early Predecessors of Isis: Cobra and Vulture Goddesses

The two oldest Goddesses of the Egyptians that evolved into versions of Isis and that have closest ties with the prehistoric Great Mother are the Cobra Goddess, *Wadjet*, who is the protector of the Lower Egypt, and the Vulture Goddess, *Nekhbet*. She is the patron deity of the Upper Egypt. They are also aspects of the Sky Goddess of the earlier, matriarchal culture during which the Goddess ruled alone, without the male consort. The Cobra and Vulture Goddesses were believed to be in possession of unlimited powers. During the patriarchal dynastic times, in spite of the advent of the divine male sons and mixed gender trinities, Wadjet and Nekhbet were still revered. Their images, the cobra and the vulture, adorned many temples and the ritual headdresses of the Kings and Queens of Egypt. These Goddesses, like Isis, were Sun Goddesses. Another Sun Goddess and version of the ancient Mother, Mut, likely an aspect of Sekhmet, was believed to be the Mother of All, but was later converted into the wife of the new male Sun God Ra, who gained dominance within the andro-centric pantheon. Like Isis herself, the ancient Goddesses Wadget and Nekhbet were believed to be absolutely essential as the protectors and the nurturers of the Pharaohs on both the earthly and heavenly planes. Therefore, they were also represented in the form of the Sacred Heavenly Cow.

Isis and Nephtys: Duality and Sisterhood

One of the closest aspects of Isis is her twin sister-Goddess, Nephtys. Both are depicted in art as winged, and their functions interrelate. Isis is always the one who is the symbol for the throne, which the pharaohs occupied as they sat on her archetypal lap; however, she is also the protector of the royalty. Both Isis and Nephtys are married to their twin brothers, Osiris and Seth. While Isis and Osiris are in love with each other, both Nephtys and Seth seem to covet the other sibling of the opposite sex. Nephtys is helpful to Isis on several occasions, while Seth represents the evil side of the divine masculine. This myth is one of the popular legends within the dynastic Egyptian legends. It also confirms, through the symbolism of the wings, the origin of Isis and her sister-alter ego Nephtys as the later version of the Paleolithic and Neolithic Bird Goddess who is the Creator and Mistress of the Sky. The Neolithic Bird Goddess, the precursor of Isis, had a number of functions according to Marija Gimbutas, including her role as the All-Giving Mother, the Creator-Regenerator of nature and all the living beings. This Birth Goddess, Life Giver, the Bringer of Death or Transforming Goddess has numerous symbols among the birds of prey, including the vulture, the owl, the hawk, and the kite. Because of her keen eyesight, the Goddess is believed to be All Seeing. According to Plutarc, the functions of the divine sister Nephtys are defined as *"the mistress of all that is unmanifest and immaterial, while Isis rules over all that is manifest and material."*[17]

Hathor: The Sun Goddess and The Sky Cow

One of the most important aspects of Isis is the Great Goddess Hathor. She is another divinity that emerged from the same prehistoric world that gave Isis her origin, and was formerly the sole Creator. Hathor was worshiped as the Sun Goddess, Snake Goddess, and also as the Sacred or Heavenly Cow. In fact, the similarities are so great between Hathor and Isis, that it is not easy to separate them, or their temples. In America Goddess Hathor is usually seen as an aspect of Isis among the followers. The Sacred Cow imagery associated with Hathor is very ancient and rooted in the matriarchal societies. At that time the Primeval Waters and the High God were perceived as female, and the nourishing flood came from the Star Studded Cow as her milk. This Hathor-Cow contained the Sky, the Sun, and the Moon. She represented the Universe, as the Great Nourishing Mother.[18] Hathor, like Isis, had a son named Horus, a symbol for the Kings of Egypt who often were represented in art suckling the Great Heavenly Cow. Pharaoh-Queen Hatshepsut and other pharaoh-queens of Egypt were also represented suckling the divine nurturing milk of Hathor; Hatshepsut was depicted suckling Hathor on the wall of the temple she had built for the goddess as her earthly incarnation. When represented in human form, Hathor, like Isis, carried the sun disc on her head between her cow horns. Like Isis, Hathor not only gave life, but also welcomed her subjects as they arrived to the realm of the dead, to be incarnated again with her help.

The Heavenly Star Studded Cow, Hathor is the Mother Sky; her son Horus, as he grows up, becomes the golden falcon, the Egyptian symbol for the Sun. He is the rising sun, who at night flies back into the mouth of Hathor and is born again each day. At night, Horus would become the Bull, or the consort of Hathor, the Sky Cow. Therefore, the blending of Isis and Hathor is almost complete, as Horus becomes Osiris. The universe of this myth is represented by a Cow-Woman who creates and nourishes her world on a continuous basis. When the male Sun God myth was later introduced, then the solar Hathor became his female counterpart. In another myth, the eyes of Hathor are the Sun and the Moon. The Snake Goddess aspect of Hathor is related directly to her solar powers, as she is the powerful fiery serpent-protector. One of the manifestations of the great powers of Hathor is her ability to be a superb shape shifter: she adopts many forms, including her manifestation as the sycamore tree. This heavenly Goddess is also the Goddess of Love, and like Isis she cares for and helps her people. Hathor is a happy and positive Goddess, and her myths do not include any personal dramas.

Sekhmet and Isis: Two Aspects of One

The beautiful and powerful Sun Goddess, Sekhmet, is easily recognizable because she is usually depicted with the head of a lioness. She is also a manifestation of Isis, and wears a Sun disc on her head. According to the myth formulated during patriarchy, Goddess Sekhmet is a transformative Goddess with a violent temper, and she can destroy and vanquish. She is extremely powerful and is married to the Sun

God Ra. She is the Shakti — or active energy, without which Ra is weak; she is also the darker side of Hathor. Ra, with the help of other Gods, has to keep her happy by appeasing her, or else her fiery temper could prompt her to kill, and scorch the earth. Her powers are increased by the fact that she is also the Serpent Goddess, an aspect that ties her to the early matriarchal heritage: Sekhmet is derived from the same primordial Mother Goddess as Isis, and her worship dates back to pre-dynastic Egypt. She has two other aspects, lioness-headed Tefnut and cat-headed Bast or Bastis, both of whom had their main center of worship and a temple at Bubastis. Their functions are similar to that of Sekhmet, but the benevolence of Goddess Bast makes her more akin to the loving nature of Isis-Hathor.

The Sky Goddess Nut

According to the popular myth of Ancient Egypt, Goddess Nut or Nuit is the mother of Isis, Osiris, Nephtys and the evil Seth. She also derives from the original Mother Goddess, and like the body of the Heavenly Cow Hathor, her feminine form is covered with the stars. She is the celestial Mother God, the creator and nurturer of the universe that includes all the Goddesses and Gods. Her body represents the heavenly realm of the cosmos. She, like Isis, controls all the dimensions of the universe, material or ethereal, where everyone transitions to after death.

Maat, Goddess of Wisdom

Goddess Maat represents a concept that is complex: she is the essence of truth, justice, balance, and the inner stability and order of the universe. She best personifies wisdom; as an aspect of Isis she is represented in a similar form, but wears a different headdress. She may be understood as the universal spirit that permeates both the physical and the heavenly realms.

Isis and the Male Gods

Isis is closely associated with several male gods that are considered to be her various aspects, including Osiris, Horus, Anubis, and Thoth. Although she usually functions as the guardian and protector of these gods, she is their underlying essence. Isis also is the primary protector of the ruling kings-pharaohs, and of the several ruling queens-pharaohs that existed throughout the long history of ancient Egypt.

The Importance of Animals as Divine Symbols of Isis

As we become familiar with Isian iconography, we realize that Egyptians were extremely respectful and grateful for the natural environment around them. The animals received a lot of attention as symbols of the Goddess Isis, as well as numerous other goddesses and gods of ancient Egypt. The genuine love that the ancient Egyptian people professed for the animals is equal to, or surpasses the affection that the Native American tribal societies have for the *four legged* inhabitants of their continent before and after the white settlers established their disrespectful attitude toward them. These affectionate and protective feelings toward the animal world resulted in an abundance of animal symbols that Isis acquired as her own totemic images. She, as an omnipotent divinity, could also become one of them: a hawk, a falcon, a cow, or a cat. These animals were respected not as the Goddess herself, but as beneficial representatives of her, or her essence. The usefulness of the animals and their contributions was highly appreciated and celebrated by the Egyptians. The animal inhabitants of the planet were seen as important, and in possession of the same rights to use the planet's resources as those of human beings. This attitude was largely due to the presence of prehistoric matriarchal traits within the patriarchy of ancient Egypt. These same matriarchal components within the ancient world guaranteed that the Great Goddesses, such as Isis, could be worshiped with fervor and affection in temples dedicated to her. The world was still seen as, primarily, the creation of the Great Mother.

This mind set toward the animals changed with the arrival of patriarchal Christianity into the ancient world. The animals were gradually stripped of their sacredness, as the new patriarchal religion determined that they were created by the male God to serve the man who stood alone at the pinnacle of all creation. The woman was not created equal according to the new dogma, but was fashioned out of a man's rib to serve him. Since then not only women, but also the animals have been suffering greatly from the mistreatments by the patriarchal order, and still do. However, the new mindset is aligning with the ideas of the post-patriarchal cultural model, an undercurrent within the societies of today. Contemporary American culture is beginning to give back to the animals some of the privileges that were taken away from them by the patriarchal past. The more benevolent partnership model, when established, will allow the animals to co-exist on this planet without becoming extinct, and will improve their living conditions. The increasing interest in the religion of Goddess Isis in America is in alignment with the population's interest in the rights of the animals who share this planet with them.

The Egyptians, who loved and respected their animals, such as the cats, embalmed them after their deaths and buried them using complex rituals for the occasion. In America today, more people own cats that any other pets, while the dogs are in second place. The dogs and the cats in America perform the all-important functions to stabilize and enrich the environments of their human protectors. They have been found to be beneficial to humans as healers: they help us relax, lower our blood pressure, and make us happier, therefore prolonging our lives. Some beloved pets are buried at special pet cemeteries, but as a rule, a grieving person that lost his or her animal does not elicit the sympathy that a person who lost a human relative does because of the still ingrained beliefs, often on the subconscious level, of the inferiority of animals. This attitude condones the habits of humans to profit from the animals on many levels. Contemporary patriarchal religions officially deny that the animals have souls and can transcend into the spiritual realm, although most people believe otherwise. There is no doubt that the old views are changing, as the feminine values of compassion and love for natural environment are emerging. Today animals often serve as symbols for the spiritual realms, and for the divine feminine spirituality.

Kyra Belán

Goddess Isis embodies in herself not only the ancient matriarchal world, but also the new values of our current millennium. Women see in her a relevant archetype, and the divine feminine within each woman's soul. People see Isis as the feminine face of their God. She is the personification of the energy of love that flows through the universe, from Mother Earth, and from each live form, whether human or animal. Goddess Isis, the loving Mother, Healer, and Magician, is worshiped by American Wicca and Pagan religions. These are the largest and fastest growing religious movements in America today, formerly only existing in occult forms to protect the worshipers from public persecutions.

7.

Kyra Belán

5

Kwan Yin and Tara: From Asia to America

The presence of Goddess Kwan Yin, Kuan Yin, or Guan Yin in America is particularly common within American population interested in cultural diversity, the New Age movement, Eastern philosophies, and the seekers of feminine spirituality. People of Asian heritage and American women who are searching for the divine feminine archetypes in order to enhance their everyday lives find Kwan Yin deeply interesting and inspiring. Many own statues or paintings of the Goddess, which are produced in the Orient and the United States by artisans and artists who replicate traditional art works of historical significance for public consumption, or create new originals. To satisfy the demand of those who like to display her images in their homes, they are mass-produced and distributed nationwide to be found in numerous gift shops, Oriental supermarkets, and New Age stores, or sold directly on the internet. Kwan Yin's presence is also apparent in the priceless collections of major art museums across the nation. Her popularity, either as Bodhisattva or a divine female, is evident within the Americans of both European and Asian backgrounds. This is due, in part, to the social movement that started in the late nineteen sixties, when flower children appeared in San Francisco, California, and started to experiment with Eastern religions and philosophies. Since the women's movement of the nineteen-seventies, interest in this Goddess increased, as women asserted themselves as individuals and discovered the feminine faces of the divinities. Kwan Yin exudes perfect femininity and beauty, and represents the nurturing and caring values that are traditional and desirable in the female gender. Since our society is going through a transformation from a patriarchal to a partnership model, these characteristics are also becoming desirable in men.

In China, Kwan Yin was known as the Wise Goddess, and was a personification of a Buddha in female form. Also called Kwan-Yin-Tien and Kwan Shi Yin, she was known to and admired by the spiritual philosophers in Europe and America since the nineteenth century. Madame H.P. Blavatsky, the historical founder of the Theosophical Society, defines her as the divine trinity: the Mother of Mercy and Knowledge, the Daughter of the Logos, the female Holy Ghost or Shakti Energy, and the essence of all three. The word Kwan-Yin-Tien means the Melodious Heaven of Sound or the *Divine Voice*, so the name is synonymous with the word *Verbum* or the Word. Therefore this Goddess of Compassion is the essence of Thought, as the Word and the Speech are the expressions of thinking. Her origins in China indicate that she is the descendant of very ancient and powerful Goddesses, such as the primordial Woman Gua, the Goddess of Tao, the Dragon Goddess and the Moon Goddess.

There are several versions of the myths of Kwan Yin, matriarchal and patriarchal. This Goddess has been worshiped in Asia for about thirteen hundred years as the Goddess of Compassion. No other Goddess or God represents the ideal of self-sacrifice and unconditional love like Kwan Yin does; her limitless compassion is like a life giving ocean: primordial, vast, timeless, and eternal. Kwan Yin herself is an archetype of a perfect nurturing, loving, and selfless woman dedicated to the wellbeing of others. Her American followers, like the ones in the East, often see her as the female manifestation of the Buddha.

My first encounter with the Goddess Kwan Yin was as a child of four. It took place while I was walking through a Chinese city that was located in a northeastern direction from the nation's capital of Beijing. In the center of a plaza I saw a huge bronze statue of a Goddess who was standing inside a lotus. She looked serene, mystical, and her long robes flowed gracefully over her elongated figure. She had a wise, peaceful, and beautiful oriental face of a Great Mother. I knew little about her, and was not able to obtain any information about her for some time, till I got older. Yet my life-long interest in the feminine archetypes, I believe, was kindled at that very moment. My visual encounters with Kwan Yin in America took place in the art museums, and the numerous specialty stores that cater to the New Age crowds. One of my most memorable sightings of the Goddess took place in the incredibly beautiful city of Sedona, Arizona: an art gallery at the town's centrally located and famous shopping center, Tlaquepaque, featured many large statues of Kwan Yin, some of which were of nearly human size. They were carved out of stone, such as alabaster or jade, cast in metal, were either polished or had a polychrome finish. The figures represented the Goddess, wearing flowing robes, and standing or seated inside a lotus flower. This impressive statuary created an atmosphere of timelessness and harmony. I examined the finely chiseled sculptures, absorbing their peaceful and pensive expressions. Yet at another gallery, located at the same shopping center, I spotted a small bronze statue of about twenty inches high, an upright figure of Kwan Yin or Guan Yin standing on a dragon. The dragon's body curved gracefully under the feet of the Goddess, suggesting undulating motion. I admired this dragon-riding Kwan

Yin: the workmanship of this sculpture was superb. But my reverie did not last long: the pricey treasure was purchased by a lady customer and whisked out of the gallery. A couple of years later, at a gift shop in Hollywood, Florida, I acquired a white porcelain statue of the Goddess seated on a lotus flower that was floating on top of nine dragons, writhing among churning waters. The statuary of Kwan Yin is often mass-produced in porcelain, wood, stone, and synthetic materials for the extensive market of American consumers. Thus, numerous versions of the Goddess, created in China, populate the stores and Oriental markets across America; many feature hand-painted porcelain versions. Her Asian following in America, particularly among the women, consists of the Buddhists and people that were born in the United States, or are U.S. citizens. The Goddess has also re-surfaced in contemporary China since the communist regime relaxed its ban on religions. However, some contemporary Chinese-American women may be apprehensive about the Goddess because traditionally she was asked for help with the production of the male offspring in China. Thus, her role was seen as the enforcer of patriarchal rules that value males over females. Currently, a better understanding of Kwan Yin's benevolent nature is conducive to a bonding between the Asian women and their powerful Goddess.

Through the centuries of Chinese patriarchal society Kwan Yin was, nevertheless, the most popular divinity. An impressive quantity of artworks, priceless today, was generated to celebrate her. She was inserted into Buddhism, like Mary was into Christianity, around eighth century C E to soften the harsh male-centered religions.[19] She was seen as an incarnation of the Buddha, born into a body of a perfect female child that grew up to be the most dedicated Savior of humankind. As the Bodhisattva, or Enlightened Being, she chose to remain accessible to help humans on Earth rather than to transcend into the realm of the total void of the Nirvana. Her devout followers abstain from eating flesh and remain non-violent, so they can be more like her in advocating love, peace and mercy. The name of this Goddess is also significant as a mantra to her worshipers, and it's meaning has been interpreted as *she who hears the weeping world.* [20]

The origins of Kwan Yin, who appeared and got established in China between the third and twelfth centuries, suggest that she is a syncretic divinity, derivative of the old matriarchal Chinese Mother Creator-Goddess, Woman Gua, who was transformed into multiple less powerful goddesses during the development of the patriarchal social structure, while Taoism retained more of its matriarchal roots. Since Chinese Buddhism was lacking a female spiritual component, its doctrine was modified to introduce the divine feminine Buddhahood in the form of Kwan Yin or Guan Yin. Her origins indicate that she entered China via Tibet, India, and other Asian countries that were primarily Buddhists at that time. Tibetans originally worshiped their Great Goddess Tara and, with the advent of Buddhism, she was incorporated into the new cult as the Bodhisattva of Compassion, Goddess Tara. Yet in the traditional Tibetan rituals Tara is still called the Mother of all the Buddhas and Bodhisattvas. According to another patriarchal Buddhist mythology, Bodhisattva Avalokita or Avalokitesvara sprang out of Buddha's eye as a ray of light, and this enlightened being was interpreted as Tara/Kwan Yin, one capable of assuming either female or male form. According to a more patriarchal version of the same myth, Avalokita shed a tear of compassion, and Tara/Kwan Yin appeared, as the female Bodhisattva of love and compassion. Chinese people visiting Tibet seemed to be inspired by that legend in all variations, naming their Avalokita and its subsequent form, Kwan Yin. Therefore, according to these legends, Kwan Yin is either a second or a third manifestation of the Buddha energy. The need for the manifestation of the Goddess of Compassion in its purest form in China added a new component to the myth, by incorporating another legend, that of Miao Shan, the pure and compassionate princess who stayed around on Earth as an enlightened being in order to help humanity. The resulting syncretic Goddess, Kwan Yin, embodied all the desired qualities of a larger than life archetypal figure, craved by the population. In Japan she was worshiped under the name of Kannon. This Bodhisattva of Compassion, as the divine active principle, and the compassionate energy of enlightenment, was endowed with immense savior power and the joy of helping human beings to succeed. In fact, Kwan Yin is believed to fulfill wishes without asking for any promises, commitments, offerings or binding agreements, while the male divinities are believed to do the opposite. The offerings that the worshipers make to Kwan Yin must not include meat, since she does not tolerate a killing of an animal in her behalf, yet would not hold it against the person if this act were committed due to ignorance. She helps everyone, including those who have sinned.

In China, even during the harshest of patriarchal times, the divine feminine was never obliterated. Besides the celebrations dedicated to Kwan Yin, Taoism worshiped its supreme Mother Goddess, the Celestial Creator, the Tao, and the Cosmic Womb. Numerous female archetypal figures, which included Miao Shan, were worshiped as the variations of Kwan Yin. The popular legends of the Goddess were developed into numerous versions, and the artworks produced reflected the nuances of these legends faithfully. Perhaps the most impressive of the visual sacred images is the Thousand Armed Kwan Yin, who thus reveals her unlimited powers; the believers see their Savior in this aspect of the Goddess. This archetype of Kwan Yin originated in Tibet as the omnipotent Tara, later to transform into Chinese divinity. People in China, Viet Nam, Burma, and other Asian countries fully expect that the Goddess will always fulfill their wishes and save them from any kind of predicament due to her boundless love, immeasurable compassion, and unlimited powers.

Besides her connections to the Tibetan Tara-Buddha-Avalokita, Kwan Yin can be traced to several ancient Chinese deities. The already mentioned Celestial Creator Goddess of Taoism can also be interpreted as Kwan Yin, and the presence of the latter in Taoist temples is not uncommon. Yet the power of Kwan Yin as the Goddess of the people of China often connects to the legends of Miao Shan. The mythical figure of Miao Shan is believed to be the earthly incarnation of Kwan Yin, and this myth has many versions. All the variations of the legend emphasize the purity of this embodiment of Kwan Yin on Earth, her Buddha nature, and her infinite abilities for love and compassion.

In one of the variations of the myth, the manifestation of the Goddess Miao Shan is born on earth as a princess. She is one of the three daughters of a King, usually the youngest. From the beginning, her wish is to dedicate herself to spiritual contemplation and to reside in the White Sparrow Convent. At first the King approved her wish, thinking that the austere life would not be in agreement with his daughter for too long, as he planned to marry her off to an appropriate prince in the near future. Time passed, and the King realized that Miao Shan had no desire to leave the convent to resume her secular life. The king became enraged, and made sure that her life at the convent was hellish and miserable: from then on she was treated with disdain, and given the most obnoxious foods to eat. When this bad treatment did not sway her, the King sent his attendants to lead her into a secluded area in the wilderness. After the party arrived in the middle of the forest, they disappeared leaving the little princess with the headman who proceeded to behead her with his sword. As the young maiden was made to kneel, and the sword was in the process to sever her head, thunder roared. The clouds parted, and a blinding ray of light enveloped the child, as a giant tiger jumped out of the sky and carried the girl into the direction of the distant hills. The tiger was a special animal, a deity of the region. He carried Miao Shan deep into Hell, where she saw many entities suffering unthinkable horrors. She pled with the Tiger God to have them released, and, unable to resist her plea, he complied. Then he brought her back into his dwelling in the wilderness, where she received a visit from the Buddha. The Buddha of Reward, surrounded by a glimmering light, admonished her to go to the Island of Putuo. This special island had the mountain of Potala or Potalaka, which was guarded by the sea dragons; therefore, her mean father, the king, would never be able hurt her. The Buddha summoned a divinity from the island to transport the girl there, where for nine years she meditated and achieved the state of Bodhisattva. Around that time she befriended a boy named Shan Tsai or *Virtuous Talent*, and shortly after she saved the son of the Dragon King from a certain death. The grateful Dragon King sent her a luminous pearl that would allow her to read the scriptures at night. The bearer of that gift was a girl named Lung Nu, or *Dragon Maiden*. The girl was so enchanted by Miao Shan-Kwan Yin that she also decided to study to achieve the status of Bodhisattva, by Kwan Yin's side. Both children, now young adults, do not age, as they are divine; they have stayed with the Goddess ever since. But Kwan Yin longed to see her earthly parents, and a few years later she visited the King and the Queen, and converted them to Buddhism.[21]

The Putuo Island is surrounded by South China Sea and can be reached by a boat ride from Shanghai; it has been known as the island of the Goddess for hundreds of years and has several temples and sacred sites dedicated to her. The devoted visitors, who include Asian and American Buddhists, arrive there to pay respects to the Goddess. This island's earlier divinity was the *Dragon Goddess*, another traditional Chinese deity to whom Kwan Yin has syncretic ties.

The largest residence of Kwan Yin in America is located in Northern California and is called The City of Ten Thousand Buddhas. Located in the northwest region of San Francisco, it has a monastery, a convent, a library, a university, and schools for the boys and girls. The city is also the center for translation of Buddhist texts. Master Hsuan Hua, a Chinese Buddhist from San Francisco, founded it. Whoever visits the complex must behave by all its rules: meditations and various rituals must be performed by the visitors as well as the resident monks and nuns.[22] Formerly a hospital, the complex has a group of buildings that is usually accessed through an architecturally elaborate Chinese style gate; it also offers to the public one of the most beautiful statues of the *Thousand Armed Kwan Yin* in America, also known as Guan Shi Yin or Guan Yin. The three major rituals dedicated to the Goddess/Bodhisattva take place there, and include the recitations from the *Lotus Sutra* and the *Great*

Compassion Mantra. The multi-armed statuary of Kwan Yin is becoming increasingly popular with the followers. However, the White Kwan Yin, a more traditional version, in front of which women used to plead for a child, usually a boy, during the oppressive patriarchal times, is still the favorite. Yet Kwan Yin figures standing on a carp, or on a dragon, are also very popular statues that are used for personal altars in people's homes across the U S A. The dragon is an archetypal water serpent, one that represents feminine wisdom and spirituality. It is an excellent symbol for this Goddess, since it also properly reflects her infinite power to help and grant wishes to all that need her.

The enormous popularity of the Goddess through the centuries among the followers, particularly the Buddhists, is largely due to the fact that Buddha Amitaba of the Pure Land Buddhism exerted his powers upon the spiritual world that opens up after the physical life within the earthly realm is over, while the Goddess and Bodhisattva Kwan Yin's powers were exerted in the physical realm and during one's physical existence. Her presence on the Mount Putuo Shan on the island of Putuo affirmed this Spiritual Being's attunement and attachment to the planet Earth, and her deep understanding of the physical world. According to the followers, she is here as the Savior Goddess; she frees people from suffering, and the mere invocation of her name changes things, improves physical existence, heals disease and opens up the possibility of abundance in life, or at least a measurable improvement. In The *Lotus Sutra*, perhaps the most popular recitation ritual of Buddhism, the miraculous powers of Kwan Yin even preempt the powers of the Buddha, thus cementing the irresistible attraction to the all loving, all compassionate syncretic Goddess. [23]

While worship in America of Guan Yin as a Buddhist Goddess is on the increase, in China and other Asian countries numerous temples dedicated to this goddess are popular as local shrines, and are also big tourist attractions for the Americans.

Tara: The Mother of all the Buddhas

Kwan Yin, the Chinese Goddess of Compassion, has a parallel divine incarnation in countries such as Tibet, Nepal, Thailand and Mongolia: as Goddess Tara; she is worshiped throughout Asia. In America she is loved and venerated by people of Asian descent, and functions as an archetype of a divine female among secular women, often on a quest of discovering their inner goddess or spirituality. Tibetan religion originally celebrated Tara as the Mother of all the Buddhas and Bodhisattvas, and as the Goddess of Compassion, and the Savior of Humanity. Less ancient patriarchal version equates Tara with Avalokitesvara. This Goddess is worshiped in the U.S. as having two principal aspects: the White Tara, and the Green Tara. There are also numerous other aspects of Tara, but these are mostly celebrated in the Orient. Images of Tara, produced through the millenniums, are often available in America in the collections of the museums, and these artworks are priceless. The reproductions of the sacred images of Tara for private individuals and personal home shrines are usually contemporary imports from Asia: mass-produced reproductions sold at the gift shops, galleries, bookstores, and the internet. Either as a painting or a sculpture, the Goddess is often shown in a sitting pose inside a lotus with one leg bend at the knee in front of the other, or in the lotus position. She can be multi-armed or multi-headed, and is also represented standing inside a lotus, holding another in her left hand. Her body is always graceful, with breasts in full view, or in a state of semi-nudity, wearing jewelry and ornate headdresses. Tara does not hide her sensuality. Recently, walking through a week-end antique market that occupied several blocks of a city in southern Florida I came across a statue of Tara that was destined to become my own: a gold plated antique Goddess about twenty inches in height. She is represented as the four-faced and eight-armed golden Goddess seated in a full lotus posture. I noticed that an eye was present on each of her foreheads and on each of the palms of her hands. I instantly was taken by the artwork, and she adorns my home, a vision of mystical serenity and beauty.

This Goddess has been around for more than four thousand years in her role as the Primal Creator and the Earth Mother of the Old World; her remote origins can be traced to India.[24] Originally she was worshiped throughout Asia, Europe, and as far as Ireland, where she still has her sacred place today and where ceremonies in her honor still take place. She is one of the most powerful deities on Earth, the original Great Goddess who was believed to be an omnipotent creator and a merciful loving Mother. By the sixth century she was assimilated into the early Buddhist traditions as the Mother of all the Buddhas and Bodhisattvas in India, and then moved on to Tibet, where she was identified with their own Mother Goddess. The patriarchal monks transformed her into a form of the Bodhisattva Avalokitesvara or Avalokita, a genderless being, also seen as a male. According to another gender reversal patriarchal myth, she was born from the tear of compassion of that Bodhisattva. However, the old myth of Tara is still accepted and celebrated alongside the new male-oriented versions. This is often the case with the Goddesses that survive and prosper under the dominator patriarchal cultures. As the mythological Buddha or Bodhisattva, Tara has been reincarnating for thousands of years in order to help the people and all the creatures she unconditionally loves. In view of the fact that the Buddhas and Bodhisattvas were usually males, she made a decision to incarnate only in female form, not the preferred male form. She vowed to use the female form till all the injustices were eradicated from the planet Earth. Tara clearly kept her ties to the old earth-based matriarchal spirituality and serves on Earth in her capacity as the Savior. She never denies her sensual and fertility aspects, thus becoming more accessible to the beings on this planet that she loves and protects. The believers-worshipers of Tara, like those of Kwan Yin, see her powers as unlimited. She stands for the concept of unity between the spirit and matter, and the energy continuum that flows between the earthly and the spiritual realms. Tara, the Buddha of Compassion, loves her physical world, which includes all the life forms. She is the compassionate and forgiving Mother, and is also celebrated as the Maiden. The devotion among her following is strengthened because of the belief that her energy creates a direct connection between the individuals in need of help and her self.

The divine energy of Tara is perceived as the *Shakti*, the active creation energy that all the goddesses of India possess. The *Shakti* energy is believed to be the female energy by the populations of India, Tibet, and other countries that worship Tara and other female divinities. This energy is called *yin* in China, and it is the energy of action and creation. Tara, full of *Shakti*, springs up into action to help her beloved people, her children. As extensive symbolism of colors developed within the visual representations of the powers and rituals of Tara, many different aspects of the Goddess also emerged. By far the two most popular versions of the Goddess among her worshipers are the Green Tara and the White Tara. The Green Tara is the Virgin Goddess, and is traditionally represented as a young or teenage woman; she provides the fastest help and relief from pain and distress. She is the Tara of active and boundless energy, the dynamic manifestation of the divine source. The Green Tara is often represented, when seated, in a posture of ease, with one of her legs extended, as if ready to spring immediately into action when her help is needed. Her skin is green, and her body is slim, well proportioned, sensual and beautiful. She wears jewelry and her body is only slightly covered with tight fitting garments. In traditional Tibetan Buddhism, Tara rescues the worshipers from their major fears visualized as tigers, elephants, or snakes, and the internal enemies visualized as anger, pride, envy, or avarice.[25]

The other very popular Tara is represented as a beautiful mother figure in charge of the life force, therefore longevity can be achieved by praying to her: she is the nurturer of life, the White Tara. Her white skin is symbolic of the purity and essence of truth, and she is particularly celebrated as the Mother of all the Buddhas and Bodhisattvas. White Tara possesses seven eyes; in addition to the usual two, she has one in the middle of her forehead, and one on each hand and foot. All these eyes represent her omnipotence. White Tara wears beautiful white garments and many jewels, which cover her sensual and shapely body, while her breasts remain uncovered. The lotus flower that she usually holds in her left hand is symbolic of her as the source and the Mother of the three Buddhas: the past, present, and future. The two aspects of Tara, the Green and the White, Tantric and Buddhist, represent perhaps the most complex archetype of the unity between the spiritual and the sensual. It encompasses an uplifting spirituality that represents deep-rooted Buddhist philosophy, the ancient religion of the Mother God-Earth Mother, and yet it is relevant to the postmodern world of the twenty-first century. Tara's roots can be presumed to go back many thousands of years, perhaps even as far as 30,000 BCE. The similarities between her and the Native American Earth Goddesses are striking and seem to substantiate a connection between the continents of Asia and the Americas. To American women Tara offers a powerful insight into their inner divine essence, and a fulfilling personal spirituality. In America, people who seek inner perfection, harmony, action, health, and longevity, or if they are of Buddhist inclination, choose to meditate upon this Goddess.

8.

6

From India: Kali, Lakshmi and Saraswati

The Hindu immigrants and their descendants brought Hinduism and, with it, the Great Mother of India, to America. India's vast territory is currently one of the few countries in the world that worships the Great Mother Goddess in all her aspects within their mainstream culture. The influence that India exerts on the religious and philosophical thinking in America is considerable. The growing population of Indian descent in the U.S. has been asserting itself in many ways. During the last few decades, Hindu people in America have formed communities, and built their places of worship that include the honoring of the divine feminine principle.

One such temple is located in South Florida in the western part of Broward County. My husband and I were fortunate to attend a ritual ceremony that took place there. I relished the harmonious chants, the flowers and fruit placed in front of the altars dedicated to various Goddesses and Gods, and the crowds, wearing indigenous garments, sitting on the floor on a large rug, with family members grouped together. Serenity, sanctity, and joy filled the building. These rituals came from a heritage that can be traced back thousands of years into the history of India when ancient bare footed adepts were intimately involved in the process of worship. The abundance of sculpture inside the temple created an atmosphere conducive to meditation; numerous individual altars displayed deities dressed in brilliant colors and shimmering gold, surrounded by their objects of symbolic significance. Like the Ancient Egyptian civilization before them, this population of the twenty-first century sees animals as symbols of the divinities and as the possessors of spiritual characteristics that match or surpass those of humans. The Sacred Cow, a Hindu symbol for the nurturing divine feminine, is astounding to the western mindset that is trained to profit from the beasts without giving them anything in return. On the contrary, the Sacred Cow and other animals, which symbolize the divine essence of beings, are cared for in India even when wealth and food are scarce. The reverence for Mother Nature and the belief in reincarnation are characteristics of the Hindu heritage that are similar to those of the Ancient Egypt, the long lasting civilization that is admired world wide, and is admired in America.

Shakti: The Universal Goddess Energy

During the prehistoric and ancient times, people of India worshiped the Mother Goddess as an omnipotent Creator. The concept of Shakti was developed over time from that original belief. Shakti represents the divine feminine active energy; she pervades everything – the universe – and she empowers all the deities, female and male. Shakti is the energy in action, the life force, the light source, the Sun, the Earth, and the life-giving nature of the physical universe. This Goddess-Source pervades everything, and other goddesses are aspects or parts of her. Shakti is also called the Devi, All That Is, and she activates the physical and the spiritual realms. The dichotomy between the heaven and earth does not exist in Hindu philosophy; therefore, the sanctity of Mother Nature and her animals is preserved, since it is not believed that the world was created at the service of humans who are entitled to prosper at the cost of other creatures. The concepts of Hindu philosophy are profound and universal; the symbols and archetypes are complex and provide human beings with the richness of spirituality that is difficult to surpass. A serious study is necessary to fully comprehend the depth of this philosophy. The resulting inner peace and vital awareness are highly beneficial to humans.

The triangle, pointing downward, represents the female divine principle in India; it also appears in the prehistoric shrines build by the hunter-gatherer tribes as far back as 3,000 B C E. There are also a number of domed shrines and dolmens that represent Mother God and have entrances that resemble the yoni, the vaginal opening or the birth passage. Numerous prehistoric and ancient figurines, images of Mother Devi, are also found in various regions of India. There are numerous vessels that represent Shakti, and the production of the vessels as symbols for the Great Goddess still continues today.[26] Numerous temples, dedicated to the various aspects of Shakti-Devi thrive in contemporary India, and the images of the Goddess, both three-dimensional and two-dimensional, abound within the Hindu culture. Images of the Goddess are produced in contemporary India; then, they are sold to local home shrines, or exported to the United States. In America they end up as private altars in the homes of Goddess worshipers, and offices or homes of the persons seeking the divine feminine as an archetype for the benevolent female values that are emerging within a contemporary culture.

A striking fact about the religious beliefs of India is that the supremacy of the divine feminine has pervaded its ancient culture since the prehistoric–matriarchal times, remaining throughout the patriarchal times when usually the Goddess gradually disappears; and it still continues on into the present. Although several male divinities have established themselves as supreme during Vedic times between the fourth and thirteenth centuries, the belief in the primacy of God the Mother continues to this day. Author Ajit Mookerjee, in his book *Kali the Feminine Force*, states that the "Evidence of feminine ultimacy is widely prevalent in India whether venerated as Nature or the life-force, as Mother or Virgin, as the Great Goddess, or as the Ultimate Reality."[27] The population of India celebrates the Goddess and her life-generating body parts such as the breasts, the pubic triangle, and the yoni or vagina; these feminine body parts are perceived as sacred and divine, and the yoni in particular is the subject of ritual veneration.

During the establishment of the Vedic tradition, besides the pre-Vedic Mother Goddess and her numerous aspects, one more Goddess was added to the Hindu pantheon, and her name is Aditi. In Rig-Veda she is defined as the Progenitor of the Universe, the Ultimate Creator Goddess, the Great Mother Womb from which everything becomes. At the same time, she is the Goddess of Light, a Luminous Sun Goddess. Devi Aditi is the Vedic counterpart of the Great Cosmic Mother, the Protector, loving, nurturing and gentle. She has the power to make anyone's wishes come true, and she is the Divine Nature; like the Great Egyptian Sun Goddesses, she is symbolically represented by the Sacred Cow. It is a fact that adoration of the sacred animals astounds those tourists who are raised within contemporary Western culture. American tourists often fail to understand why a mere animal could be considered sacred due to the fact that their own mainstream male centered religions are not kind to the beasts of the world, regarding them as creatures born to serve. In India, on the contrary, Goddess Aditi as The Sacred Cow is perceived as the archetypal Nurturer and is loved and appreciated by the grateful population. The *sacred cows* roam the streets of the cities and are cared for and fed, even when food is scarce. Like in Ancient Egypt, there is also a Goddess in India that specializes in being the Sun Goddess as her principal function, and her name is Suria. She is another form of the Shakti energy.

It is a scientific fact that all life is initiated in female form, and that in human and animal worlds, half of these beings remain female while the other half eventually become male in the womb, and are born as such. In Hindu religious philosophy, this primacy of the female gender has been recognized since time immemorial and still is today, many centuries after the male Gods appeared on the scene during patriarchal times. Within Hinduism, a woman is seen as a sacred representative of the Ultimate Creator, the All That Is, the Primal Shakti, or the Great Mother. She is the first source and not the *other*, as the dominant patriarchal religions of the West postulate. Within these western religions, the male is the prime recipient of the divine favoritism. In Hinduism it is Shakti that is the primal and powerful energy, particularly embraced in the Tantric religions of the East. These Tantric religions of India now also have a following in America. Within the Tantric rituals, a woman represents all the women as the supreme divinity; she embodies all the aspects of Shakti Devi. During the ritual she is the active force, primordial and divine, while the male partner represents the passive force. Hence all the male Gods exist because of the active life-energy of Shakti, and they cannot survive without her; she is the original energy of the universe.

Since the male gods are manifestations of Shakti, the Tantric Goddess, they yearn to be in touch with the female aspect of themselves. In fact, they are included in the many aspects of the Great Mother – Shakti – All That Is. The primal role of the divine feminine within the Hindu religion explains the existence of the numerous female images in Hindu art. According to Mookerjee, "The feminine power has been given expression in a multitude of female figures, both in sculpture and painting, in which the emphasized forms of the breasts, belly, hips, yoni, and thighs seem an incarnation of the rhythms of the universe. From the Medieval period, Tantra's bold depictions of the themes of sexual union, menstruation, pregnancy and childbirth restored to sacred art essential symbolic figurations virtually suppressed by taboo."[28]

The three aspects of the Hindu Great Mother, like elsewhere in the world, include the Creative force, the Nurturing or preserving force, and the Transformative force. The Transformer or the Destroyer Goddess of India, who has migrated to America and who represents well this particular *Shakti*, is Goddess Kali. This extremely complex Goddess is celebrated in India as the archetypal image of the Mother of birth and death, simultaneously the giver of life and the devourer of her own creations: a thousand other ancient religions portray her in the same manner.[29] Seemingly the original Goddess-Destroyer, she was described in Tantric writings as the beginning, the creator, the protector, and the destroyer of all.[30]

Goddess Kali

Goddess Kali, Kali Ma or Kalika is the Hindu Triple Goddess of Creation, Nurturing, and Transformation. Her beginnings are extremely remote and belong to prehistory; she is currently worshiped mainly in her aspect of Destroyer/Transformer, or the Dark Mother. Goddess Kali is the archetypal figure that is the Birth and Death Mother who is both the giver of life and its destroyer. This kind of Goddess can be found in many ancient religions, but in contemporary India people understand the complexity of the life cycles that Kali creates and they fully accept her as their Creator. Kali stands for life, for the totality of existence, and for the flux of both the matter and the life force, the continuing activity of becoming. As the Great Mother, she constantly creates and is the Mother of all the Gods and Goddesses. The Tantric writings proclaim her as the original of all the manifestations, birthplace of all the divinities, the infinite, and the beginning. The Supreme Kali is the possessor of unconceivable power; she is the Beginning, Creator, Protector, and Destructor.[31] The Great God Vishnu, of immense powers himself, is subservient to Kali Ma and regards her as the material manifestation of all change, life, and destruction as "the whole Universe rests upon Her. From Her are crystallized the original elements and qualities, which construct the apparent worlds. She is both the mother and the grave...the gods themselves are merely constructs out of Her maternal substance, which is both consciousness and potential joy."[32] The primal energy of Kali in all her aspects appeals not only to the fervently devout Hindu population, but also to many Americans. This Goddess has an extensive following in the United States as an archetype of the Primordial Mother. The oldest existing official writings about Kali date around 400 CE, appearing in *Devi Mahatmya*. According to that legend, Kali first appeared from the brains of the supreme Goddess Durga. Both have many similarities and can be interpreted as two distinct aspects of the same Mother God. The ability of Kali to destroy evil forces is unsurpassed, her energy is boundless, infinite, and imbued with unlimited Shakti powers; no other force can be compared to that of Kali. She is the manifestation of the one Devi that can assume a limitless amount of power and numerous goddess and god forms.

The representations of Goddess Kali follow established traditions. She is commonly represented in her destroyer aspect, as black skinned and in the nude, in both sculpture and painting. Often, her red tongue is sticking out of her mouth, giving her a threatening look, also emphasized by the necklace of skulls hanging around her neck. She is often seen dancing on top of the reclining and passive body of Siva or Shiva, as she is the active energy that gives him divine life. In America, one can find images of Kali sold in specialty shops, grocery stores, or food marts run by immigrants from India, or by their American-born descendants. Some of the two-dimensional kitsch art can be plugged into the electric socket for attractive visual effects, symbolically underlining the powerful active energy of the Goddess. At Hindu temples in America, both Kali and her Mother Durga are usually represented as three-dimensional figures: Kali in her aggressive Destroyer aspect, and Durga, holding her weapons, usually riding a tiger or a lion.

The attraction to Kali in contemporary America is due in part to a deeper interest in understanding the Hindu philosophy: its principle of female primacy within the order of the universe, and Kali's representation of the universal principles of the cycles of life, death, and transformation. More than that, Kali is time itself. As the Mother of Time, she controls our lives and the evolution of the physical universe. As she constantly creates, she also destroys and transforms. She is the awesome force of change within our physical universe.

One of the earliest myths about the Goddess dates about 600 CE, and describes her as the most formidable warrior Goddess. Since she is invincible, she often attracts worshipers who come from the impoverished people of lower casts. She is born of the angered brain of the Goddess Durga, a War Goddess herself, and that makes Kali an aspect of her mother. Kali and her numerous female divine assistants vanquish the Devils; Durga-Kali is invincible, and there is no male god that can win a battle against either one. Kali is also an aspect of Parvati, a protector Goddess and the wife of Shiva. A gentle divinity, she protects the families and stabilizes their lives. Therefore, Kali assumes the role of the aggressive, dark side of Parvati.[33] We can glean how the Great Goddess of Hindu religion manifests herself in a multitude of aspects, each serving a purpose, and exercising her creative powers that control the universe. Probably the most fearsome aspect of Kali is her manifestation as Time, a constant flow that brings birth, growth, decline and death. Facing Kali allows an individual to confront every aspect of life, including the last stage, that of the decline and, ultimately, unavoidable death. But the philosophy of Hinduism includes the belief in reincarnation, so with every death there is a new birth for the individual involved. This may be another reason why Kali attracts such immense following.

The popularity of this Goddess in India is awesome, and she is also one of the most revered divinities by the population of Indian descent living in the United States. American women see in Lakshmi an archetype, since they are interested in discovering the divine feminine within their own and world cultures. Commonly known as the Goddess of prosperity and well being, Lakshmi is also Shakti, the Great Goddess whose active energy pervades and creates the whole universe. According to Vedic literature, Lakshmi is celebrated as the giver of beauty to the world, as well as power, royal qualities and, above all, abundance, wealth, and physical health. These are the gifts that Sri Lakshmi bestows on her followers, and she is strongly associated with wealth and royal powers.

Although Sri Lakshmi is connected with these desirable qualities, coveted by rulers and by gods, she is also perceived as the Goddess of Nature and the Goddess of Agriculture, qualities that indicate her remote and primal origins within the pre-Vedic times, and align her with the prehistoric Great Mother. She is luminous, radiant, and is the Sun Goddess who rewards with an abundance of natural growth and fertility, and the Moon Goddess who watches over the cyclical nature of life. Lakshmi is venerated by the rural population of India as the Earth Goddess that ensures the fertility of the soil. Extensive symbolic iconography surrounds the Goddess to explain her powers in visual language. Traditional symbols of Lakshmi include the lotus, a flower from which she emerges, either seated or standing. The lotus represents her perfect beauty, her ties to the vegetation cults of prehistoric times, and her immense powers as the creator. In India, the lotus flower or *padma* is connected to and obtains its strength from the primordial waters, and is symbolic of fertility and life.[34] Lakshmi originates and constantly re-creates the universe, including the life giving Mother Earth, where her presence is necessary for the abundance in the physical world to proliferate. The Goddess is the apex of all that is beautiful within the universe, and she embeds the very essence of beauty and harmony into all of her physical creations.

The lotus also represents Lakshmi's powers over the endless world of spirituality that operates within the infinite realms of extra sensory dimensions. Sri-Lakshmi, seated in a lotus, represents her dominion over the spiritual cosmos, the iconography that she shares with Guan Yin, Tara, and all the Buddhas and Bodhisattvas. Another important symbol of Lakshmi is the elephant. Elephants are seen as special and sacred in India, and they represent spirituality. According to the legend, they had wings in earlier eras and resided in the sky as the clouds that generated rain and, therefore, helped create abundance in nature. Lakshmi is often depicted in art with these sky elephants. Ganesha, who is an elephant-headed god, also provides abundance and, therefore, is often shown in art seated next to Sri-Lakshmi. According to some legends, he is her child. The elephants, like Lakshmi, represent royal powers.

Lakshmi's mythology is extensive and has many variations. She is tied to several important male gods, and some of them are believed to be her husbands. Soma, the god of vegetation, often is associated with Lakshmi and collaborates with her to create abundance in nature. In some sacred texts she is the wife of Dharma, the god of Virtue; other texts make her the wife of God Indra, a God-King, and it seems appropriate that the Goddess of Royal Power is wedded to him. Kubera, the God of

Vegetation and forests, is also considered to be her husband, and together they endow people with wealth. However, God Vishnu is most often associated with Sri-Lakshmi as her consort. In that role, Lakshmi represents the faithful and dutiful wife, and has the most traditional role within Hindu religious legends as she often acts as his companion. Yet she is the Shakti of Vishnu, and as such plays central role in the process of creation. Although Vishnu participates with Lakshmi in the plan of creation, she is the one who actively creates the universe, while he passively contemplates her activities. She is the creator, while he maintains the order.

In her native lands the worship of Lakshmi requires that many rituals be performed in her temples, while numerous festivals are also enacted. One of the most popular festivals of the Goddess takes place in autumn, and corroborates her significance as an important divinity of agriculture and harvest. These celebrations of Sri-Lakshmi as the giver of abundance in nature compliments her other attributes as the giver of prosperity, wealth and royal power. In Orissa, where women of India enjoy a matriarchal society, Sri-Lakshmi is worshiped on a mound of fresh grain. The belief that Lakshmi, like Demeter of ancient Greece, controls fertility and abundance in nature, and in her absence planet Earth remains barren, underlines similarities and interconnectedness between the two religions.

The presence of Lakshmi in America is on the rise. Women see her as an important Creator-Goddess archetype that represents the embodiment of female power and creative energy. This creative energy pervades not just the heavenly realm, but also the entire physical universe, and celebrates female presence within nature, and within each individual woman. The divine persona of Lakshmi represents feminine spirituality and creative principle that can empower self identified women who do not wish to be treated as second-class individuals within the male dominator establishment.

Saraswati

Goddess Saraswati is another divinity popular in America that arrived from India. Her initial appeal to American people is most likely due to the similarities between her attributes and those of Goddess Athena. In her country of origin, Saraswati, although the daughter of the Great Mother, is directly associated with the Vedic cosmic river. According to the legend, these archetypal waters have come down from the skies into the earthly realm, populating the lands with abundant life. Saraswati is seen as the possessor of the power to generate storms, fast running rivers and large bodies of water, such as the lakes and oceans. In fact, the divine energy of Saraswati is triple, as it pervades the celestial, atmospheric and earthly realms.[35] These sacred waters of Saraswati are purifying, and are permeated with spirituality: they are cosmic waters. The worshipers expect Saraswati, as the body of sacred waters, to free them from all impurities. Saraswati is also seen as the Healer: healing rituals were performed at the banks of the river Saraswati, which cannot be found today within the physical world. However, the waters still flow within the mythical rivers of Saraswati, not just in India, but also in other parts of the world, including America.

Water symbolism seems to be the earliest connection to Saraswati; she later morphed into the Goddess of the sounds, including music. Vedic hymns describe her as the Goddess of the words, speech, thinking, and wisdom; thus, the similarity to Goddess Athena is significant. Saraswati is the Great River of flowing energy of wisdom and thoughts. The expressions of our thoughts through the sounds of the words aptly explain the deep psycho-spiritual meaning of this Mother Creator. Saraswati is the flowing and limitless body of spiritual waters that fill the cosmos with the fertility of wisdom that translates into thoughts, words, and the sounds of music. The worshipers of Saraswati are purified, inspired, transformed and reborn by performing rituals that include the submergence into the waters of a river from which they emerge as newly reborn.

During the post-Vedic times Saraswati is described as the Goddess of speech, learning, wisdom, and culture, including the arts. She is represented as playing a musical instrument in her role as the Goddess of Music. Above all, however, Saraswati is celebrated within Hinduism as the Goddess of Speech, or The Word. Therefore, she is the Goddess of Thought, a fact that is critical within the Hindu thinking. She is present whenever words are spoken, and pervades every human mind. Since speech is seen as primal in the development of a culture within Hindu philosophy, Saraswati's importance is underscored by her constant presence, including during a state of meditation. The use of the mantras is central to a successful spiritual development, and therefore, such sounds as Om are seen as the universal sounds of creation. Saraswati is manifested through the sound, which explains her as the Shakti-Mother, or the primordial act of creation.

9.

Kyra Belán

7

The Native American Goddess: Mother Earth, Thought Woman

Our car was headed south, back from a visit to the Grand Canyon, its awesome beauty still lingering in my mind: my husband and I were driving toward the city of Sedona, another place known for its red mountains and rock formations of stunning beauty. For millennia, the Native Americans regarded the Grand Canyon and Sedona as sacred sites. These sites were visited for ceremonial purposes, but no permanent dwellings were built there. The Native Americans only visited the area to worship Mother Earth and her divine essence. These expanses of land were used as places for meditations, vision quests, purifications, sun dances, prayer, or other sacred rituals. The invading *white man's* civilization, on the contrary, brought with it disrespect for Mother Earth, nature and the animals. The reverence for the planet, normal to the Native American nations, was foreign to the people whose philosophy was based on a dichotomy or two distinct realms: the heavenly as superior, and the earthly as inferior. According to Western religious philosophy, everything physical was associated with the feminine, seen as the inferior gender. Consequently, Mother Earth lost its lofty status. The white settlers promptly began to populate and build upon the sacred grounds that formerly belonged to Native Americans. Today Sedona, one of the biggest tourist attractions in America, is growing every day as a city, and so are many other former sacred sites that have become densely populated tourist attractions, or industrial developments that generate environmental damage.

In the past, however, Native American civilizations did not subscribe to Western philosophy that condones the deterioration of natural environment. On the contrary, the indigenous people loved their Mother Earth passionately and used her resources carefully and sparingly. America was first populated by largely peaceful tribal societies, the majority of which were matriarchal or matrilineal, and did not wage wars. The spiritual world was seen as important as the physical, represented by planet Earth herself, as the body of the Mother Creator. She was appreciated and prayed to as the provider of all life: she was the Mother of the animals, or the *four-leggeds,* who, in the eyes of the indigenous tribes, were respected and entitled to the same privileges and rights on the planet as human beings. Women were respected by the indigenous culture for their abilities to create human beings out of their own flesh, and they were believed to be the embodiments of Mother Goddess. Traditionally women inherited the lands and the cattle, passed along from a mother to a daughter. Children inherited their mother's last names and the clans of the mothers; they still do to this day.

Today Mother Earth is still viewed by the tribal nations as the Great Mother Creator, and is the subject of rituals and ceremonies. These celebrations of the feminine principle in nature and society is re-emerging during the new millennium and attracting members among American population who are interested in social issues: ecological, philosophical, and eco-feminist. People, particularly in western states, such as California or Arizona, plan their vacations so they can attend the many events and workshops that allow them to learn about the Native American cultures and their philosophy of earth-based spirituality that includes the divine feminine. This seems to fulfill their needs for the healing of tensions, stress, and mental problems, aggravated by a society that separates humans from nature and from each other. These activities also help restore a connection between human beings and their planet. American people often seek this elemental connection through their visits to the Native American reservations and viewing or participating in their rituals, visiting their sacred sites, and learning about their culture, and the arts.

The state of Arizona is currently the home to the legendary white buffalo, sacred to the Native tribal cultures. The sacred beasts are located at a small ranch, near the city of Flagstaff on highway 180 en route to one of the most beautiful features of Mother Earth: the expanse of the Grand Canyon. The white buffalo is a symbol for the divine woman who appeared to the Lacota tribes in the form of the White Buffalo Calf Woman. She, according to the legend, brought the peace pipe to the Lacota, in addition to her teachings of ritual practices and the sacred wisdom. When my husband and I approached the ranch and pulled into the parking slot, the sacred beasts could be observed behind a wire fence. We walked toward the enclosure, anxious for a close-up look of the animals. There were several of them. The first White Buffalo, a female, Miracle Moon, was born in South Dakota of parents whose color was brown; she became the matriarch of a family of white beasts. The buffalos' coats were of a light, creamy color; they were born white, but as they aged, the color got darker. I watched them graze peacefully, occasionally glancing at the visitors with curiosity. I noticed that many visitors left symbolic gifts near their fence. It was obvious that the guests took the White Buffalo prophesy seriously: the comeback of these animals during our times was seen as the proof of the re-emergence of the Native American Nations, and an omen for future peace and harmony on Earth for all humanity. I sensed from the demeanor of the animals that they were content, and aware of their importance to the visitors. The calm beauty of the environment created a backdrop of harmony. Even though the space that enclosed the buffalo was not large, it allowed enough room for the animals, and the visiting crowds provided them with entertainment or distraction. The friendly beasts seemed to inspire the visitors, Native Americans and Americans alike.

The birth of a white buffalo is a rare event. These buffalo are not albino, but possess natural light coloration. One previous recorded case of this kind of birth occurred in 1933, yet the best known is that of the birth of Miracle. She was born on August 20, 1994 and died on September 19, 2004 near Janesville, Wisconsin. As the news of Miracle's birth spread (I read about it on the internet), thousands of people visited the small farm – they were allowed to see the animals by the owners who were sympathetic to the Native American beliefs in the spiritual connection of the buffalo to the myth of the White Buffalo Calf Woman. To the Native Americans, the presence of the white buffalo among them meant that the future was changing in a positive way. It was a message telling them that the Americas and the world had increased chances for peace, harmony, and wellbeing. This white buffalo calf also symbolized the rebirth and strengthening of the Native American cultures.

The small ranch near Flagstaff, the *Spirit Mountain Ranch*, had seven white buffalo: the original, Miracle Moon, followed by Rainbow Spirit, Arizona Spirit, Mandela Peace Pilgrim, Sunrise Spirit, Spirit Thunder, and Chief Hiawatha. These symbols for the spiritual presence of White Buffalo Woman are not all female; a couple of them are males. The first buffalo, a female, Miracle Moon, was born on April 30, 1997 and the youngest was born on May 16, 2005, according to the official website. The legend predicted that the appearance of the white buffalo signaled that Mother Earth was releasing beneficial energies. The Divine Savior herself, White Buffalo Calf Woman, is expected to return to Mother Earth in either a spiritual or physical form to re-enforce harmony, peace, and the rebirth of the Native Nations. The owners of the ranch, however, due to health problems, moved their buffalo to Arizona from South Dakota in December 2001, thus enhancing the spirituality of the state of Arizona. However, the ranch was sold, and the white buffalo were relocated to a ranch in central Oregon, owned by Cynthia Hart-Button. She happens to be the descendant of Sitting Bull, and honors the legend of White Buffalo Calf Woman.

Buffalo Calf Woman or White Buffalo Calf Woman

According to the Lacota-Sioux religion, White Buffalo Calf Woman is a messianic figure. She brought with her ceremonial knowledge, wisdom, and a lasting future for the Lacota and other Native American Nations. The prophecy of the Buffalo Woman, according to the popular legend, is at least two thousand years old. She first appeared to two young hunters-warriors who departed from the sacred Black Hills of South Dakota to hunt the buffalo. Soon they spotted a group of buffalo at a distance in an open field, but one buffalo was running toward them as if wanting to give them a message. Then it dissolved into a large white cloud-like shape, which turned into a white buffalo calf. As the buffalo calf got closer, it shape shifted into a beautiful Native American young woman who wore a white buckskin dress and carried a bundle. As she approached the two hunters, she sang a melodic song.

One of the young hunters was immediately filled with evil and disrespectful thinking regarding the young woman. She told him to step forward, and when he did, a black cloud instantly enveloped him. When the cloud dissipated, only a pile of white bones, as if bleached by the Sun, was seen on the ground. The other young hunter kneeled down to the ground and began to pray. The beautiful Buffalo Calf Woman was still standing in front of him. He saw that she seemed to radiate golden light out of her body, a being of incredible beauty. Entranced, he heard her melodious voice: "Go back to your people and tell them that in four days I will bring to them the sacred bundle." Overwhelmed and elated, the warrior returned and advised his people of her future arrival.

In four days the elders, the leaders, and all the people gathered in a circle, waiting. They saw a large cloud come down from the sky; gradually, a white buffalo calf's shape separated from the cloud and stepped toward them. They saw the calf shift into a form of a beautiful woman holding the sacred bundle wrapped in buckskin. As she walked toward the people they heard the most beautiful sounds put together in a song; then she stepped into the circle and offered them the bundle. She stayed with the tribe for four days, instructing them about the significance of the sacred bundle as a symbolic and ritual object. She also taught them the wisdoms of life and the sacred ceremonies that would deeply improve their existence. The ceremonies included the keeping of the soul rite, the healing ritual, the purification ritual or sweat lodge ceremony, the naming of a child ritual, the adoption ritual, the marriage ceremony, the sun dance ceremony that celebrates the divine feminine and the Corn Mother, and the spiritual ritual of the vision quest. The White Buffalo Woman, in her role as her people's Messiah-Savior, also taught them many songs, and many traditions that they still practice today. She instilled in her people respect and love for the sacred land, Mother Earth, and promised them that as long as they kept her teachings alive, they would have their land to take care of and pass on to the future generations. She made a promise to return to bring balance, harmony, and purity to the world. The sacred Buffalo Woman left the same way she came: she returned into the circle, then exited it, while shifting into the white buffalo calf, and then becoming a cloud, ascending up into the sky. This Lacota myth is similar to the Christian legends that include the Ascensions of Jesus, Mary, and Mary Magdalene.

On the land of the Sioux there is another, expanded version of the prophesy. In the ancient times, when the indigenous nation was not divided, there was a woman known as the Mother of Life. She devoted her existence to caring for the people, and because of her actions, she was respected and loved. When the enemy attacked her village, she covered a mortally wounded child with her body for protection. When she was gravely wounded herself, she, in spirit form, followed the child into the spirit world where she continued caring for the infant. While there, she asked the Great Spirit: Why must people fight instead of resolving their differences peacefully? She then decided to come back to Earth in order to teach her people the ways of peace, harmony, and perfection. Her new arrival on Earth was as the Savior-Teacher in the form of the White Buffalo Calf Woman.

The bundle that the Buffalo Calf Woman left with the people contained the sacred Peace Pipe, which is always guarded and has been passed on from generation to generation for about two thousand years as a symbol for continuity of the cycles of harmony, peace, and abundance in nature on planet Earth. The use of the pipe is dedicated to keep the communication between the people as truthful and harmonious within the circle of life. It is kept at a secret location on the Cheyenne River Indian Reservation in South Dakota. The prophesies of the White Buffalo Woman include the birth of a white buffalo as an indication that her next visit is not too far away. Therefore, the actual birth of a white buffalo at a farm is an event of importance in the lives of the Native Americans and is taken as an indicator of the upcoming era of harmony, peace, and reverence for Mother Earth. White Buffalo Calf Woman is the mythical Divine Daughter, the messenger of the Goddess/Great Spirit, and the Savior-Heroine of her people. Her teachings are paramount to the lives of the Native people of America in the new millennium.

The non-Native American population often misunderstands the messianic character of the Buffalo Calf Woman since they have been acculturated within a patriarchal society, which traditionally does not credit women with such important roles. In the book, titled *Mother Earth Spirituality* by Ed McGaa, a Native sage by the name of Eagle Man refers to this problem:

"Indian people feel that it is very poor manners to refer to the Buffalo Calf Woman's appearance as a myth or superstition. Indians do not scoff at the story of the Israelites fleeting Egypt when the Great Spirit in order for the Jewish people to escape the pharaoh's pursuing army parted the Red Sea. We have been told over and over by Christian missionaries that a man, born of a virgin, died, rose again three days after the death, pushed a big stone back from his tomb, and then ascended into the spirit world. An Indian would consider it poor manners to make fun of this spiritual story, especially if it is a part of the people's spiritual history. Similarly, the Jewish people would be offended if the story of Moses' vision questing on the mountain were called a myth, especially the part where the Great Spirit appeared to Moses and gave him special instructions, or commandments, on living and conduct.

Perhaps it is because our spirit guide happens to be a woman that the male-oriented missionaries find it difficult to grasp. That is very sad. It is their loss. Is it not obvious that women are the peaceful ones? Does not the animal world exhibit this observation? The males fight far more than the females do. Since the dawn of recorded history, it is the men, not the women, who have plunged into war. Womankind is half of the human world, but most importantly, women are the peaceful ones, and in this new era, it is the most peaceful ones who will bring ultimate harmony."[36]

The prophesy of the White Buffalo Calf Woman is very much in tune with the realization among both Native and non-Native American people that it is crucial to keep the teachings alive as we face destructive human behaviors by the proponents of wars, consumerism, and global warming due to environmental damage that is being inflicted on our one and only Mother Earth. Thus, those people who envision a positive future for our planet and its children revive and respect this prophecy today.

Another divine woman, from more recent times, populates the legends of many indigenous tribes, including the Dakota, the Cree, and the Crow. Her name is Omaamikwe. She gifted her people with the large drum to be used at the gatherings or pow-wow meetings, and the rituals of wisdom, songs, and dance that are enacted during these gatherings. The large drum is a symbol for the heart beat of Mother Earth, and the hand drums are her children. While the hand drums existed for many centuries, the large drum appeared around two hundred years ago. Omaamikwe, the mystical daughter of Mother Earth, was among the members of her tribe who were captured and massacred by the white men in uniforms, but she managed to escape. She ran and plunged into the river where she hid by staying under the water for four days, breathing through a reed. While in the water, the Great Spirit advised her to go to a certain place in the forest and walk to the top of a hill. As she got out of the stream and walked right though the camp of the American soldiers, none could see her. Following her instructions carefully, she took some food to placate her hunger and started to walk toward the area indicated by the Great Spirit. She reached the exact location, and, after a brief rest, dropped some food and tobacco on the surface of the Earth to honor the spirit beings and the ancestors. She remained on site for four days; then, she suddenly saw a beautiful round object descend from the sky and land next to her. Omaamikwe also heard the voice of the Great Spirit within herself; it instructed her in detail about the purpose, the wisdom, and the rituals of the drum. Her newly acquired wisdom included all the songs and the dances, and all the drumbeats that were necessary for a gathering. It became clear to her that she must pass this knowledge to her people. Consequently, The Big Drum Society was formed, and the gatherings of the tribes resumed, gradually increasing to become large nation-wide events.

Omaamikwe, like the White Buffalo Calf Woman, is a teacher who has imparted ritual knowledge to the tribes. She is the divine Daughter of Mother Earth, and a Messenger or the Messiah to her people.

Changing Woman

The Navajo people have a legend about their Creator Goddess called the Changing Woman or Estsanatlehi. She is believed to be either second or third generation divinity, the daughter of the divine pair of Mother Earth and Father Sky; another myth tells us that the First Woman and the First Man discovered her on the top of a mountain. According to yet another legend, she spontaneously appeared carried by the rays of light onto a mountaintop. Changing Woman first created all the animals, and then the Navajo people by rubbing her skin off her body. She also represents the cycle of life, or the seasons. She changes from a young maiden to a mature woman, and to an old wise woman; then she returns back to the age of a young maiden, representing the cyclical patterns of nature. Mother Nature is reborn in the spring, matures in the summer, and offers abundance in the fall, while becoming dormant and frozen in the winter. Changing Woman is Nature, and she is also Mother Earth. She is often associated with her sister Goddess or alter ego, the White Shell

Woman. The White Shell Woman represents similar powers, and both have divine children. The cycles of the Moon and the menstrual cycles of women are also celebrated through the honoring of this Goddess. Kris Waldhherr, author of *The Book of Goddesses*, states that Changing Woman's teachings, designed to help her people function successfully during their cycles of life on earth, "are presented within the *Blessingway*, a group of essential rituals and chants" that Changing Woman is believed to have authored. The songs and the ceremonies that make up the *Blessingway* are used for weddings, childbirth rites, and other happy occasions in the life of the Navajo. Each *Blessingway* takes place for several days and includes many songs, prayers, and ceremonial baths in yucca or cactus suds. Pulverized flower blossoms, cornmeal, and pollen are spread upon the earth to bless it and to bring good fortune.[37] Waldhherr also mentions that a very important ritual in each woman's life is called *Kinaalda*, and it celebrates the coming of age of young girls. This affirming ritual, a part of the Changing Woman's teachings, takes four days. The young girl is honored by being attired in a special costume, her hair brought back to suggest a resemblance to the divine Changing Woman herself. A large cake, symbolic of Mother Earth, is baked for the final section of the ritual; as it is prepared, the song is sang as follows:

" With Beauty before me, I am traveling,
 With my sacred power, I am traveling,
 With beauty behind me, I am traveling,
 With my sacred power, I am traveling."[38]

The Corn Mother

The Corn Mother is celebrated and loved by many tribes in North America. Her worship also extends to the civilizations of the Mayas and other tribal societies in Mexico. To the Keres of New Mexico and to many other tribes, she is one of the principal Goddesses. She is believed to have created people out of corn. She governs the spiritual life of the people, as well as their existence on the other plane after their deaths. Through her authority, the chief and the mother chief together govern the people.[39] Within the native mythologies, the Corn Mother is often a part of an important group of Goddesses, which may include the Changing Woman, the Thought Woman, or the Spider Woman, among others. There are many versions of the legend of the Corn Mother, some of which I will discuss in this chapter.

Selu, the Cherokee Corn Mother

Selu is the nurturing aspect of Mother Earth, as symbolized by the corn she provides for the people. She is also the Wise Woman. Like the Changing Woman of the Navajo, this Goddess creates corn out of her own body, and she appears in the legends as the mother or the grandmother who nurtures her offspring and dies only to be reborn as corn plants over and over, providing a limitless abundance of food for her people. Selu is often celebrated by the contemporary Pueblo Indians of the Southwest as Santa Clara. Christianity vigorously suppressed all the Native religions since the days of conquest of the Americas by European invaders; therefore she was camouflaged as a Christian Saint.

Blue Corn Maiden

Besides the Corn Mother there are many tribal legends about the Corn Maidens. The Pueblo legend about the Blue Corn Maiden echoes the Mother and Daughter religion of the ancient Greek people of Europe known as the Mysteries of Demeter and Persephone or Kore; her role is similar to that of Kore, the creator of Nature in springtime. The Corn Maiden gave delicious blue corn to her people all year long, and they were very happy and well nourished. She was also very beautiful and gentle. When she left one day to gather firewood, she encountered the Winter Katsina, a supernatural being who immediately fell in love with her and talked her into moving with him into his cold iced up house. He kept her inside, while going out and constantly icing up the world, but she managed to get out by prying the door open and breaking the ice into pieces. Outside she encountered the Summer Katsina not too far away in the woods. He also fell madly in love with The Blue Corn Maiden, and the feeling was mutual. Soon a dispute started between the two Katsinas and was eventually resolved by having the Blue Corn Maiden stay with the Winter Katsina half a year, during which the Pueblo people starved and suffered, and the other half a year with the Summer Katsina, during which time the Corn Maiden could, as before, provide for them generously with the abundance of delicious blue corn. Therefore the Pueblo people experience hardships half the time, and abundance during the rest of the time. The female divinity of this tale represents the holy force that is always positive, while the male divinities can go either way: positive or negative. The love and respect for the sacred feminine is obvious within this indigenous culture: this Native American Kore is the beloved daughter of Demeter, the Earth Mother.

The Corn Goddess

The Corn Goddess, worshiped by the Iroquois, is the direct descendant of the Earth Mother, and, as her daughter, represents the principle of regeneration and rebirth in nature. While the Earth Mother is, within her body, the creator of everything, her daughter the Corn Goddess is the one who generates all the abundance in nature, including a generous supply of corn. Again, this myth echoes the European myth of Demeter and Kore of ancient Greece, and the parallels are clear. The Mother–Daughter divinities are present in the myths of the Iroquois, Shoshoni, and Hopi, among other tribal cultures. The Corn Goddess is represented as a beautiful young woman who may also appear as a trinity of sisters: the divine spirits of corn, squash, and beans. According to some legends the Corn Goddess sprang out from the Primordial Mother Goddess, the predecessor and creator of Mother Earth.

Chicomecoatl: Corn Mother of New Mexico

In Mexico Goddess Chicomecoatl or Seven Snakes is celebrated as the Goddess of Maize and of abundance in general. She is also the Goddess of Fertility, and during the times of harvest is celebrated as the Fire and Sun Goddess. She possesses a shield that is a symbol of the Sun in traditional artistic renderings, which is her attribute as a Sun Goddess. Chicomecoatl is prominent in Mexico; to the tribal societies she is the goddess of abundance, nourishment, maize, and water, another essential energy that brings life to fruition and sustains all the life forms on Earth.

Our Grandmother

This is a version of the primal creator Goddess that is worshiped by the Shawnee. She lives high in the sky and watches her children, the people, through a window in the sky. She gave them fire, and taught them how to cook and how to make baskets. She is also associated with the lunar cycles. When one crosses to the other side – the realm of the dead, the deceased person always enters a place that Our Grandmother rules. She is the creator of the physical world, the spiritual plane, and of all other divinities including the Corn Goddess.

Spider Woman or Thought Woman

The Spider Woman, also called the Thinking Woman, Thought Woman, Tse che nako or Tse'itsi'nako, is worshiped and revered by many Native American Tribes, including the Navajo, the Pueblo, the Anasazi, the Laguna, and the Keres. She is at the central core of the creation process, or the one who creates from a central source: she is the source of all creation. She is symbolically connected with the dream catchers, the web-like wall hangings that Native American people create for their own ritual use, but; due to their popularity with the general public, they are available for sale at reservations, gatherings, selected stores, and on the internet. The dream catchers come in many sizes and are visually very attractive. Many people collect the dream catchers as artworks, while others keep one or more at their houses for good luck, often hanging them over their headboards so their dreams would be positive. The dream catchers are believed to have powers to materialize dreams into reality, and to forecast propitious futures. Native Americans of Mexico often perform peyote rituals in honor of the Spider Woman. As a source from which all life sprang and within which each part of the web strands is interrelated, the Spider Woman, as the creator of the web of life, is perceived as the Goddess who spins each person's destiny.

The Thinking Woman, Thought Woman or Spider Woman is the primordial divinity; therefore, at first only She existed. In the beginning there was no light or dark, no heaven or earth, no spirit, no time, no wind, no sound, no water, no fire; there was only the Thinking Woman, pure thoughts. Then her thoughts created the universe and its four directions (east, west, north, and south) and the galaxies, the planets, and the earth surrounded by a layer of sky, the Blue Planet. Then Spider Woman created more thoughts, and the planet got covered with the oceans, rivers, and vegetation; the animals also appeared out of the Spider Woman's thinking. Finally, the humans appeared. To create them, the Spider Woman used clay that was red, yellow, black, and white, thus creating the four races of people. The thoughts of the Spider Woman that create everything are pure and clear, like the ultimate vision quest: full of unlimited power, unlimited love, and unlimited beauty. Since usually religions of the indigenous Americans are richly polytheistic, Thinking Woman also created supernatural divine beings: other important Goddesses and Gods, as aspects of herself. She also created the two major Goddesses of the Pueblo people: the Sun and the Moon. After that, she created the Star People to illuminate the Earth better. As a manifestation of the omnipotent Great Goddess, the Spider Woman, The Sand Altar Woman, The Spider Grandmother, The Corn Goddess, the Weaver of Destinies, the Spirit that Pervades Everything – she is the universal and unlimited creative force, not surpassed by any other Native American Goddess or God.

Paula Gunn Allen describes the Keres version of the Spider Woman, The Spider Grandmother, in her well-known book, *Grandmothers of the Light*:

> "Spider Grandmother, the major deity of the Keres, is weaver and thinker: She thinks therefore we are. Though she is "supreme" – the thought sounds wrong put in those terms and read from a Western perspective where "supreme" means king or pope or dictator – she is not alone. There isn't an "only" just as there isn't a beginning as such. Surely, the Western mind inquires, something comes before her, something made her. Surely the universe has a beginning, and an end. But like their stories, which go on and on, Indians seem to believe that life itself does not have endings. And, if that is so, then what use is there for the beginnings?
>
> I have depicted Spider Grandmother as a Great Goddess whose medicine power is so vast (or whose own being is so vast and focused) that she brings thoughts or ideas into being. In my sense of her, she is akin to Wind. Indeed it is said that she is Wind's Grandmother. That is because she makes movement and from movement all else derives."[40]

Thought Woman or Spider Woman represents the female creative force, and she is also seen in abstract terms, as The Source, All That Is, or the Divine Energy. This way of reasoning is inherent to the Native American spiritual philosophies. The variety of legends or myths about the divinities co-exist with strong underlying philosophies that see the cosmos, the galaxies, and the Mother Earth as infused with the creation energy of the divine force of the Thought Woman. They see the underlying energies that unify all reality much clearer than the general public within the Western culture does. This reality is explained through story telling, an important form of art within all the American Tribal Nations. The story of Thought Woman or Spider Woman, or her creation myth, is explained by Leslie Marmon Silko, a Laguna/Pueblo Indian, in her book *Yellow Woman and a Beauty of Spirit*:

> "So I will begin, appropriately enough, with the Pueblo Creation story, an all-inclusive story of how life began. In this story, Tse'itsi'nako, Thought Woman, by thinking of her sisters, thought of everything that is. In this way, the world was created. Everything in this world was a part of the original Creation; the people at home understood that far away there were other human beings, also a part of this world. The Creation story even includes a prophecy that describes the origin of European and African peoples and also refers to Asians."[41]

It is interesting to note that first two beings that Thought Woman or Spider Woman creates are her two sister-goddesses who become her co-creators. This is a form of a Goddess Trinity; there are similarities between this Pueblo trinity and the many triple Goddesses found in the mythologies of the prehistoric and ancient civilizations as well as some contemporary female trinities that constitute the beliefs of some parts of the world, usually located where matriarchies, or matriarchal characteristics within a society still exist, or a partnership model of a society is newly emerging.

Sun Woman

The Cherokee Tribe has a legend about their Sun Goddess. She is Sutalidihi, also called the Six Killer. Her solar power is great, and she functions as a measurer of time, space, and life spans; she is also the implementer of justice. The Sun Woman induces harmony and balance on earth, and a friendly peace-generating behavior in humans and all other beings. Six Killer lives in a house beyond the sky in the east. She travels from east to west and back during each day. Her original location was rather close to the surface of the earth, and she had to adjust it six times, each time higher, till she reached the seventh height – or the highest place in heaven from which she dispenses her benevolent sun rays to warm up nature and people, and to make their lives prosperous and abundant.

Sun Woman also called Sun Living in the Day, as a young girl had a brother who professed amorous intentions toward her while visiting her at night so she would not recognize him. She discovered and disclosed his identity, and he had to flee. His name was Sun Living in the Night, but after the incident, he became the Moon, and since then the two siblings always stay as far as possible from each other.

The Sun Woman later had a daughter, called the Sacred Flame. On several occasions her enemies, the jealous priests, had connived to get rid of her daughter and could not succeed, but their last attempt produced results. They turned into serpents and monsters by using magic, and killed Sacred Flame. Saddened, Sun Woman abandoned the earth by going into the heavenly realm with her daughter's ghost. The earth became barren, cold, and the plants, animals, and people were quickly dying. Feeling sorry for her subjects, Sun Woman came out of her hiding; now she spends about half the time with her subjects, while the other half is spent in the other world with her daughter. This myth has similarities with the ancient Greek mythology of Demeter and Kore, the mother-daughter Goddesses who were worshiped there for about three thousand years. The archetypes of this Western cultural heritage are similar to many Native American myths about the mother and daughter divinities.

The Goddesses of the Huichol

The Hiuchol, Native Americans that reside in Mexico near Jalisco and Nayarit, are well known for their production of colorful fiber artworks. They worship many goddesses who are the aspects of the Great Mother; these divinities define their entire lives. The Huichol perform peyote rituals as a part of their religious ceremonies. Peyote, which is a hallucinogenic, is a form of a cactus plant that grows in the desert of Mexico and some adjacent states of the U S A, such as Arizona. The Huichol people are an agrarian matriarchal society. There are many similarities between the Huichol culture and that of the Mayan, Aztec, and Toltec civilizations. The Earth Goddess is another name for the Great Mother Goddess of the Hiuchol people. Her name is Nakawe, and she is perceived as all-powerful. In fact, all the Goddesses of the Huichol represent different aspects of Our Great Grandmother. Like the Aztec

Goddess Coatlicue, or Chihuacoatl the Serpent Woman, she appears with numerous snakes as her symbols. Numerous cultures of the world revere the serpent as the symbol of the earthly powers of the Mother Goddess, and the myths of the serpent applies to the Huichol as well.

Goddess Coatlicue, Mother God of the Aztecs

My first encounter with Goddess Coatlicue of the Aztecs happened in Mexico City during the decade of the nineteen-eighties. I was visiting the *Museo Antropologico de Mejico* and discovered a monumental statue, made out of stone, of this serpent skirted Goddess. The statue was most extraordinary: the Goddess was represented in an abstract manner: a combination of a woman, a serpent, and an eagle. All these elements were skillfully recombined into one abstract figure carved in the round, yet a closed form. She displayed the most unusual head: two profiles of serpents facing each other. This magnificent creation, probably carved by several sculptors, is different from other depictions of the Goddess in stone or clay. The rest of the statues represent female forms: divine women wearing skirts of serpents. I was so moved by this sculpture that I started to investigate the myths behind this Goddess, and was compelled to create artworks in her honor. The first work of art was a 12' 6" colored pencil drawing, where three images of women appeared to be emerging from what was my artistic reinterpretation of the statue of Coatlicue. The drawing later became a centerpiece for two different site-specific installations, complete with ritual performances that included dance movements and chanting. The first installation was an eighty-one foot long serpent coiled into a spiral in the center of the gallery's floor, and the second had an annular shaped double-headed fifty-five foot long serpent spread on the floor of the art gallery's space. Both floor sculptures were shaped as plumed snakes, and were created out of clay, sand, rocks, and feathers.

The mythology of this Aztec Goddess was a pleasant surprise: her iconology defines her as the Mother Goddess-Creator. According to this myth, Coatlicue created the galaxies, the stars, and the solar system, including the Sun and the Moon. These celestial bodies, to the Aztecs, were also Goddesses and Gods. Then she proceeded to create everything else within the physical world of the planet Earth, including the people. But not everything went well: when she got pregnant with her new son, Huitzilopochtli, her other divine children decided to kill her. Instead, he sprang out of her full-grown and killed them. They are now a part of the firmament staying at some distance from the earth. Coatlicue is the giver of life, and she also is the taker of life or transformer. She is the nurturing Mother Earth, and her favorite daughter, Tonantzín, is the loving and caring Earth Goddess that reminded the Natives of the Christian Mary, the Mother of God. The acceptance of Mary within Mexico by the Native people was largely due to the presence of Coatlicue worship. In America, Coatlicue is important as the mother of Tonantzín, also known as The Virgin of Guadalupe. Both divinities are understood as the aspects of each other.

Kochininako or Yellow Woman

The Pueblo and other western Native Americans celebrate another Goddess whose story is interesting because it does not fit into the conventions of Christianity or other Western myths or traditions regarding women. Since the Native American women feel equal to men – they have a female creation myth of the Thought Woman that places them in a position of total equality – this story is natural to a civilization that comes from a point of view of the sanctity of nature, the absence of the original sin, and the sacredness of female sexuality. Yellow Woman is named for the color of the East rather than her actual skin color, and she is one of the many divinities thought or created by the Spider or Thought Woman and her two sisters. Kochininako is said to be beautiful, which means to the Native Americans that both her body and her spirit were in harmony with nature and other beings. Because of the drought, she had to walk far to the east to find water for her husband and children. She found a spring, but it was clear to her that the waters were churning; she then saw a very handsome man that turned into a buffalo. She fell in love with him and rode him back to his herd. Because of this encounter, the buffalo allows the hungry Pueblo to feed off the herd. On other occasion, the Yellow Woman met the Whirlwind Man, and their affair resulted in twin boys. Ten months later, she returned to her husband and the twins grew up into great warriors, which benefited the tribe. In both cases the exuberant sexuality of the Yellow Woman produces great benefits for the tribe and is seen as an asset.[42] Female sexuality is valued differently in a society where the male paternity is not an issue. Women's fertility and sexuality are celebrated through this Native American myth.

Goddess Pele of Hawaii

The islands of Hawaii are rich in a matriarchal heritage that includes myths, legends and worship of many female divinities. The original Creator was believed to be an energy field perceived as either gender-neutral or female. She is known as Mother Goddess Uli. The Goddess as Mother Earth is known as Haumea, the creator of the islands and the many Goddesses and Gods. She can also be equated with Goddess Uli and is believed to be the Creator of the people of Hawaii. Her most important two children are, without a doubt, the sister Goddesses Pele and Hi'iaka. Both are necessary for the well being of Hawaii. Hi'iaka, who is the younger sister of Pele, and whom Pele raised as her own, is the Goddess of The Creation of Vegetation, animals, and people, and is essential to the exuberance and abundance in Nature, including its procreation. Hi'iaka is the Goddess of Resurrection and also hula dancing. Her older sister Pele is the better known of the two goddesses worldwide and has many similarities to the transformative divinities from other cultures, such as Hindu Goddess Kali.

According to another popular myth, Goddess Pele is the great granddaughter of the original Creator Goddess Uli, granddaughter of Great Sky Goddess Papa, and daughter of the Earth Mother - she came out of her mouth as a flame, and became the Goddess of Fire and Volcanoes. She, however, is an Earth Goddess, as she creates the landmasses from the lava of the exploding volcanoes. She appears to humans in the form of a young and beautiful woman, or in the form of an old, wise woman. At times she appears in the form of a female dog. Goddess Pele purifies the islands of unnecessary materials or mental debris, and awakens the use of people's natural gifts or talents. She guides her worshipers to higher levels of wisdom. Through the sacred energy of Pele they can attune to the phenomenon of transformation and transmutation in nature and in their lives. Pele's awesome powers are believed to be unlimited. Pele and all the other Goddesses of Hawaii are all aspects of the same divine source, the Great Mother, also known in Hawaii as Uli or All That Is.

Mother Earth

It is clear that the original inhabitants of America have respected and worshiped the divine in women, and appreciated the feminine and maternal qualities in human beings for thousands of years; they are still ahead of the rigid and exclusive patriarchal vision of the conventional spirituality. Even after living through oppression of their original spiritual beliefs for centuries, Native American understanding of spirituality is rooted in the philosophy that respects our physical environment as much as the spiritual or heavenly realm. Patriarchal religions always place the spiritual realm above the physical, thus promoting disregard for our planet, Mother Earth, but in Hawaii, due to its strong matriarchal roots, the awareness of the divine feminine is fully present within the physical realm, and the universal creator is often visualized in female form.

10.

Kyra Belán

8

Mary Magdalene

Emerging in the new millennium as an archetype of the sacred feminine, Mary Magdalene is today the subject of increased interest and reverence. Recent research has uncovered the Gnostic Gospels and the incomplete Gospel of Mary Magdalene, and the new revelations of the early Christian faith, alongside the accepted and church-approved Christian doctrine, have become a part of the popular knowledge. All the sources indicate that a much stronger presence of the divine feminine existed within the early Christian religion. Since the general public is no longer satisfied with the traditional legends generated by the Christian establishment for nearly two millennia, these new findings are gaining acceptance among the believers. The fact that early Christianity, although patriarchal, was more open to the inclusion of the divine feminine, is now common knowledge. The desire to return God the Mother to her rightful place alongside the glorified God the Father has become strong among the American population. Not only the Christian Mother of God is popular among the believers, but other mythological females of Christianity have also re-emerged: Sophia as The Wisdom, The Holy Spirit as the Divine Feminine, and Mary Magdalene as the Apostle to the Apostles and the Bride or spouse of Jesus.

For centuries, Mary Magdalene was believed to be a prostitute, due to the fact that Pope Gregory I (c. 540 - 604), also called Pope Gregory the Great since he was the most influential of the medieval popes, mislabeled her as a sinner by amalgamating two different passages from the official Gospels during the sixth century. Since the celibate church fathers resented and often disliked women, they assumed that a woman who is a sinner must also be a prostitute: Magdalene was presented as such by the voices coming from the pulpits all over Europe, bringing this misogynist approach with them to the Americas and all over the world wherever Christianity was practiced. It took many centuries, till 1969, for the Vatican to issue an official retraction. The clergy usually ignores the papal retraction; they continue to preach this degrading myth about the Magdalene. Yet adoration of Mary Magdalene, together with a longing for her presence persists, clearly not supported by the church. During the medieval times in France and other European countries, Mary Magdalene was worshiped as the divine female. The historical fact that the traditional Christian church was, for many centuries, distorting and obscuring the role of Mary Magdalene demonstrates the enormous fear that this patriarchal religion fostered against this sacred feminine figure. The fear of Mary Magdalene has deeply affected the church fathers for centuries, as they continued her vilification at a relentless pace.

The misogynist culture of the clerics of orthodox Christianity, which is devoid of the divinity in feminine form even today, is a direct result of the history of persecution of women by the church. Exactly how deep the fear of the feminine is ingrained in the official Christian doctrine is still open to a debate. However, due to the recent research, historical facts are surfacing to corroborate that it was extremely important for the Christian priests to keep the false image of Mary Magdalene in place.

As the clergy of Christianity frequently re-edited the Gospels, the sacred feminine was gradually expunged from the official church-approved Bible. Very little information can be found on Mary the mother of Jesus, even less on Mary Magdalene. However, the following facts on the Magdalene are still present in the existing Gospels: she was the first person to see and to communicate with the resurrected Jesus; she was the one that Jesus loved the most, even more than his apostles or other followers. According to the apocryphal Gospel of Philip, they were jealous of his affection toward her. Mary Magdalene loved Jesus; she funded and promoted his endeavors and his group; she was his companion, probably his bride or wife, and the mother of their child. Therefore, she represents the sacred feminine to his sacred masculine, continuing the tradition of thousands of years of religions that worshiped the Goddess alongside the male God after patriarchy first appeared as a social paradigm after it dethroned the Great Goddess, venerated as the sole creator for thousands of years.

The role of Mary Magdalene has re-emerged, and it is clear to those that read the scriptures in an unbiased fashion that in the New Testament she is the Apostle to the Apostles. After the death and resurrection of Jesus, she was originally pre-destined to lead the emerging Christianity. According to Margaret Starbird, Lynn Picknett, Laurence Gardner, and others, she, together with her entourage, moved to southern France, where she resided for at least thirty years preaching her form of Gnostic Christianity. Surely her model of the then new religion was closer to the original version that Jesus himself espoused. After the crucifixion and death of her beloved, she was the first one to claim to see him resurrected, and to communicate with him. This represents an important part of the myth of Mary Magdalene. She contributed a great deal to the Christian Doctrine, as it is known today. It is important to recognize that Magdalene is the one that originally proposed the myth of resurrection, a critical component of the Christian faith.

A healthy portion of the Christian population of the new millennium believes that she is the apostle to the apostles, a position that Jesus wanted her to have after his departure from this world. Yet, there is more to this archetypal figure that has been relentlessly maligned by the Christian priests for so many centuries. In *Secrets of the Code* author Dan Burstein states: "She is mentioned twelve times by name in the New Testament. She is among the only followers of Jesus to be present at his crucifixion and she attends to him after his death. She is the person who returns to his tomb three days later and the person to whom the resurrected Jesus first appears. When he appears, he instructs – indeed, he empowers – her to spread the news of his resurrection and to become, in effect, the most important apostle; the bearer of the Christian message to the other apostles and to the world. All of that is according to the officially accepted New Testament accounts."[43] Then, why did the church fathers, through the centuries and even today so viciously malign this sacred figure of the New Testament? Her very presence in the Bible raises numerous fundamental questions about the very foundation on which Christianity stands. Due to the new emergence of Mary Magdalene as the sacred archetype and as a primal character within a universal myth of the balance between the divine feminine and masculine, the public is interested in learning more about her. This phenomenon of the new millennium is not really new; its emergence into the public consciousness with a renewed force is an indicator that we are undergoing a change of mind-set. This change has been effectively fueled by the research done by the pioneers in the studies of Mary of Magdala, such as Margaret Starbird or Lynn Picknett. The recent bestseller novel by Dan Brown, *The da Vinci Code*, first published in 2003, has also contributed to the cause.

A Conspiracy or Complacency?

The vicious untruths that were circulated about Mary Magdalene for centuries by the church fathers can be best described as a conspiracy of awesome proportions. The majority of the population of Europe during early and medieval Christianity was illiterate, and those who could read were not allowed to read the Bible; these people were used to accepting the interpretations of the clergy without questions. If that failed, there was always another path for the church fathers to take – to brutally repress and forcibly eliminate those who deviated from the accepted version of Christianity. These repressive activities by the leaders of the church, often assisted by the rulers who had vested interest, include the mass executions of the Cathars, the Knights Templars, and the ruthless burning of thousands, or even millions of witches by the Inquisition. In each case, their crime was simply a disagreement with the version of Christianity that was promoted by the church at each particular time in the history of that religion. Throughout its history of nearly two thousand years, Christianity has very effectively functioned as a patriarchal religion that oppressed women. Even today women are not equal to men within the Christian church; most variations of the original Catholic model still do not allow women to become priests, to preach, or to be promoted to the position of the head of their church. Through the centuries, many rules and regulations were created to limit the power of women within and outside the church. The reasons for these rules can be reduced to two main issues: the divine or God is seen by the church as only masculine, and the apostles approved by the church are all male. But who is to blame? Certainly not Jesus, who loved Magdalene and wanted her to be his successor. It is also likely that she was a co-founder of original Christianity.

Why do you love her more than all of us?

In the Gospel of Philip, a well-known apocryphal gospel, there is a passage that merits our attention and dispels any questioning regarding the mutually loving relationship between Mary Magdalene and Jesus. It may be the reason why the church fathers decided to include this gospel in the apocrypha, or those gospels and writings that they deemed less acceptable than the four sanctioned gospels and the Revelations. This passage describes the discontent of the apostles regarding the relationship between Jesus and Mary Magdalene:

"Christ loved her more than all the disciples and used to kiss her often in the [mouth]. The rest of the disciples were offended by it and expressed disapproval. They said to him, "Why do you love her more than all of us?" the Savior answered and said to them, "Why do I not love you like I love her?"

Yet during the sixth century, Pope Gregory I declared Mary a sinful woman, seemingly confusing her with another woman mentioned in Luke. Soon thereafter the church fathers routinely referred to her as a prostitute. Even after the Vatican corrected this error in 1969, the priesthood continued to label her as a fallen woman either due to their habit, or to their desire to keep women in their subservient place. Looking at this through the perspective of time – fourteen centuries of vicious and degrading labeling of a woman who could have served as a positive archetype for women and men – does make one wonder whether it was perpetrated with a specific purpose in mind.

Mary of Magdala does not seem to be from the town of Magdala – it did not exist at a time. Her name most likely means tower, as she was originally seen as the strength of fledgling Christianity. According to Starbird, Pincknett, Gardner, and other authorities on Mary Magdalene, she is also Mary of Bethany, and her brother is Lazarus. She financially helped support the new religious movement, and there are indications that she came from the lineage of Benjamin, and probably spend some time in Egypt, perhaps while Jesus was also there. Mary was familiar with the religion of Isis and may have practiced Goddess worship; this was not a contradiction at that time, since the divine feminine existed within early Christianity. She has been mentioned in the gospels as the woman who anointed the head and feet of Jesus on two separate occasions with spikenard, a very expensive perfume-oil, a ritualistic approach used in ancient Egypt and the rest of the ancient world as a part of the nuptial rite of sacred marriage, or *hieros gamos*. A closer look at the scriptures regarding the marriage at Cana indicates that the marriage ceremony could have been that of Jesus and the Magdalene. Therefore, Mary Magdalene represents the divine feminine to the divine masculine Jesus. According to the prevailing legend, after the death of Jesus and his resurrection, Mary had to leave the country to protect herself and her female child Tamar (or Sarah) from the ire of Peter, who particularly disliked her and saw her as a competition. She and her retinue ended up in southern France, where she lived and preached her version of the Gospel for thirty years till her death around 60 C E. There are over 150 churches dedicated to her worship in France; a number of them have the statues of Black Madonna, considered to be miraculous; they represent Magdalene, and are also associated with Goddess Isis and Mary the Mother of Jesus.

The Sacred Ritual of the Anointing

There are many who believe that Mary of Magdala and Mary of Bethany are the same person. If so, Christian mythology clearly continues the custom, established since antiquity, of the duality of the divine as both feminine and masculine. Mary of Bethany anoints the head and the feet of Jesus with a very expensive perfume-oil, spikenard. This act is performed twice, and it has a ritual, symbolic and sexual connotations. Yet it is also deeply connected to Christianity; the term Christ comes from the Greek term Christos, meaning Messiah. The word itself, according to Picknett and Prince in their book, *The Templar Revelation*, means the Anointed One.[44] Thus, through this ritual, Jesus became the Messiah. If the baptism of Jesus is to be considered as an equally important event, then all those who were baptized by John the Baptist would also become Christs, which is not the rationale favored by the church. Therefore, the unique and ultimate ritual performed by Mary Magdalene was the anointing ritual; it made Jesus a Christ, or a Messiah. The fact that a woman performed this act created an awkward situation for the misogynist church fathers. Therefore, it was critical for the Church to discredit her. But according to Mark, Jesus himself realizes the importance of the ritual:

Verily I say into you, Wheresoever this gospel shall be preached throughout the whole world; this also what she had done shall be spoken of for a memorial of her.

The authors of Templar Revelation noted that the church did not place emphasis on either the baptism of Jesus at the beginning of his life, or the anointing rituals by Mary Magdalene at the end of his life, even though both are significant events. They have noticed that there was often a process by which selectively some statements by Jesus were deemed as important, while others were less so, at the convenience of the Church that promoted certain ideas and obscured others. It is, however, clear that those who performed the important rituals were undeniably the authorities within the new religion. "For though a baptizer and an anointer *bestow* authority – in much the same way as the Archbishop of Canterbury conferred the regal status on Queen Elizabeth II in 1953 – *they themselves must have had authority to do so.*"[45]

The anointing ritual dates back thousands of years to a time when matriarchal characteristics within the social systems were either predominant or extant. Then it was customary that a king or a ruler, in order to be such, had to be first anointed by a priestess who represented the Mother Goddess such as Inanna, Astarte, Ishtar, or Isis. This priestess-queen, therefore, transferred the sacred female divinity – through her actions and her physical body – into the king, who only then was entitled to become the ruler of the people. This process between the high priestess and the king was known as *hieros gamos*, or the sacred marriage. Only after the ritual was the king empowered; without the ritual, he was believed to be void of power and divinity.

The sacredness of the feminine as a tradition of thousands of years has been almost totally obscured during the last two thousand years by the interpretations of the church fathers that gradually shaped the Christian doctrine into a misogynist model. The idea of the sacred feminine is still unacceptable to the orthodox Christian religions. However, the sacred feminine was routinely celebrated during the matriarchal times of prehistory and antiquity when the *hieros gamos* or the sacred marriage was celebrated as a ritual to induce the fertility and abundance in nature.

Mary Magdalene assumes the role of the Goddess in the Gnostic Gospels as an aspect of Goddess Sophia and as Mary Lucifer, the Bringer of Light, or the Sun Goddess. This, of course, clearly ties her to Goddess Isis, herself a Sun Goddess, and to numerous Goddesses or aspects of the Great Goddess that were worshiped at that time or during ancient and prehistoric times. Early Christianity had various groups or sects of people who differed from each other in their beliefs. The sect that produced the Gnostic Gospels was much more favorable toward women and worshiped the divine feminine in the form of Sophia or Wisdom as complimentary to Jehovah or the Word. Also, during early Christianity, the Holy Spirit was believed to represent best the divine feminine, and not the masculine. Therefore, the symbol for the Holy Spirit, a dove, was borrowed from the older goddess-worshiping religions. It was a symbol for the Goddess Aphrodite and numerous other female divinities. The bird, in many forms, can be traced to prehistoric times as the symbol for the Mother Goddess and is often found among the artifacts of the prehistoric cultures. The worship of Mary Magdalene as the sacred feminine on earth, the counterpart of Jesus as the sacred masculine, was maintained for many centuries. In Europe Mary was particularly sacred to the people in France, since according to the legend she moved to southern France during the first century and resided there till the end of her life, preaching her own brand of Christianity. Numerous shrines dedicated to the Black Madonna were her centers of worship.

The Black Madonna is represented as dark skinned, but with Caucasian features. This seems to strongly relate the Magdalene to Goddess Isis. And the darkness of the features seems to allude to the fertility of the earth; all the ancient goddesses, like the Great Isis, were believed to have unlimited powers as Earth Mothers, generating the abundance and fertility in nature, as well as fertility in humans and animals. Mary Magdalene, like Isis and the Virgin Mary, was represented seated on a throne with a child on her lap. Her first child, an offspring of Jesus, is believed to be Tamar or Sarah Tamar, and was a female; in a society that normally celebrated only the divine male offspring, female child was not desirable. However, in the ancient world, the celebration of the divine female child was not unusual; the best example of the mother and daughter goddesses is the existence of the mystical and extremely long lasting religion of Demeter and Persephone (or Kore). Also, the celebration of the sacred feminine is common among the cultures that developed outside the western traditions, such as Asian or Native American.

Mary Magdalene, like Jesus, was the heir of goddess-centered religions, archetypes, myths, and symbols. Many of the legends, miracles, and rituals from ancient religions, particularly those of Inanna, Ishtar, Astarte, Demeter, and Isis, were incorporated into the legends about the activities that Jesus undertook and which Christianity adopted as its own: the baptism by water, symbolic-ritual raising of the dead, transformation of water into wine, miraculous cures and other. Traditionally the goddesses, such as Isis, were known as Saviors of humanity, a title later attributed to Jesus. The Magdalene, when worshiped as a Goddess during early Christianity, possessed monumental powers in the eyes of her faithful and was seen as sacred, mystic, and magical; therefore, Magdalene was also seen by her faithful as the Savior of humanity. Other Isian powers attributed to Mary Magdalene included those of a healer and a protector. Mary Magdalene was perceived, like Isis, as the primeval *All that Is* by her Gnostic followers.

From the Gnostics to the Literalists

The Roman emperor Constantine, a worshiper of the Sun God Mithra, initiated the battle against the sacred feminine in Christianity. Constantine found it politically advantageous to proclaim Christianity as the official religion of the Roman Empire since he desired to usurp the position of Jesus and to become the Savior Christ figure himself. He felt that in order to achieve this, Jesus had to be proclaimed a God and a part of an all male trinity. This, he felt, would free the legend of the Messiah or Christ figure for his personal use. The historical facts prove that this last mission of self-adulation did not stick; it was deleted shortly after his death. However, his forceful intervention not only changed Christianity, but also reinforced the war against the divine feminine, and further facilitated the oppression of women. Even though after his demise he lost the battle of becoming the new Christ, he had set up a pattern of misogyny that the church continued to promote for the next two thousand years that profoundly affected the roles of women within the new religion and the society.

Constantine, noticing the increase in Christians within his empire, declared Christianity the official religion of Rome in 313 C E. At that time, Christianity consisted of many groups who had very few similarities between them, with the exception of recognizing Jesus as their prophet, or Messiah. The initial groups were roughly divided into Gnostics, who believed in the divine within each human being, and the literalists, who were better aligned with the version of Christianity promulgated by Peter, which emphasized the idea of following him and his subsequent successors in Rome, and accepting their ideas. In order to organize the new religion toward his aims, Constantine got together the Council of Nicaea in 325, located within the geographic confines of today's Turkey. The emperor ordered his bishops to come up with a dogmatic statement about the nature of Jesus and to define the direction in which the religion would go for centuries to come. From this council, the more orthodox and literal version of Christianity emerged, supported by the emperor. Jesus was declared divine, the son of God, and the concept of the all male trinity was established as a part of the official version, leaving out the teachings of the less sexist Gnostic doctrine which accepted the female aspect of God. After much bickering, the Council issued its official statement or creed:

"We believe in one god, the Father Almighty, maker of all things visible and invisible, and in one lord Jesus Christ, the Son of God, the only begotten by his father…" The third aspect of the trinity was only mentioned briefly: "and in the Holy Ghost".

The creed also affirmed the belief in the resurrection of Jesus, thus completing all the essential elements of the Roman version of Christianity, which would become the mainstream literalist Christianity. It is important to point out that the Council of Nicaea did not establish the gender of the Holy Spirit, but the assumption that the Holy Ghost was male soon became embedded into this patriarchal version of the creed. The Council of Nicaea was considered very important, since the Emperor himself, determining the path that Christianity would take for many centuries, supervised it. It worked out a list of canons or rules by which the Church should be run. These included the admonition that the church priests and bishops should be men, and that they should stay away from women, presumed a bad influence on the clergy.

The Gospels and Mary Magdalene

It is a fact that Jesus himself never wrote anything, and that the earliest possible date for the first gospel written by someone is at best 70 C E or, most experts agree, about 200 C E or later. The four gospels, eventually accepted by the church fathers as the canonical gospels, are the most literalist of the Christian writers' production, and the most misogynist: they constitute the official dogma of the church fathers. But did the apostles originally write these four gospels? According to Acharya S., Waite, and others, all four gospels were penned around 170-180 C E coinciding exactly with the timeline when the supremacy of the Roman church was established, embracing the literal orthodoxy. The original versions of the gospels were written in Greek language. According to Waite, the oldest gospel was published by a Christian Gnostic Marcion in the Greek language and served as a model for the canonical four. The Gospel of Luke was written around 180 and is a compilation of writings from dozens of older manuscripts. The Gospel of Mark was the second oldest and was probably written by an orthodox Roman convert to Christianity whose first language was Latin rather than Greek. Although many scholars surmise that the Gospel of John was the latest, Waite places it as third and argues that a non-Jew for the purpose of the establishment of the Roman Church wrote it. The latest, the Gospel of Matthew was written in Greek around 200 C E and it is the most favorable toward Roman domination of Christianity. The stories in these four gospels often contradict each other, according to Wheless, author of *Forgery in Christianity*:

"The so called "canonical" books of the New Testament, as of the Old, are a mess of contradictions and confusions of text, to the present estimate of 150,000 and more "variant readings" as is well known and admitted."[46]

There are many other gospels and writings rejected by the Roman church fathers that were less orthodox or literalist, or were clearly Gnostic, including a gospel attributed to Mary Magdalene, and possibly written by one of her disciples. The Gospel of Mary, a non-canonical scripture, unfortunately has been partially destroyed, with only eight pages still extant. However partial, it is a noted example of the Gnostic trend, when an individual is assumed to have a spark of the divine in her/himself, and is encouraged to search for and find the sacred within. Another non-canonical gospel is the Gospel of Philip, where Mary Magdalene and Jesus are featured as the divine couple. The archetypal dual divinity embodied in Mary Magdalene and Jesus is evident in this gospel, and has ties to the well-known divine couple of antiquity that preceded them, Isis and Osiris of Egypt. Together with their child Horus, they formed a mixed gender trinity of Mother, Father, and Child. Since the archetypal legends about Mary Magdalene and Jesus tell us that they had a child, Tamar, this Christian trinity followed a tradition that has been there for thousands of years, and was appealing and familiar to the original Christians. This strongly female aspect of Christianity was suppressed by the church fathers, dedicated to exterminating any traces of the sacred feminine within the new Christian cult.

The suppression of the non-canonical writings persisted through centuries. The church fathers were always horrified of the possibility that the existence of the divine feminine within original Christianity would become known. The bishops knew about the marriage between Mary Magdalene and Jesus, and her motherhood that resulted in the birth of their daughter. That is why they constantly had to "vilify her memory."[47] Nevertheless, during medieval times, numerous clerics, monks, nuns, and academics persisted in worshiping the divine feminine through the archetypal figure of Mary Magdalene, her predecessor Sophia, the Gnostic Goddess of Wisdom, The Virgin Mary as the Christian Goddess, and the Holy Spirit as the female component of the trinity. Various writings on the subject appeared, were published, and the legend of the divine feminine persisted. The magnificent twelfth century philosopher, artist, and mystic, Hildegard of Bingen in her book, *Scivias*, speaks of Maria-Sophia. Her images feature Sophia as the Bride, and as the Cosmic Mother, a female aspect of God.

The symbol of the Holy Spirit is the Dove, the same symbol that was used in earlier times to represent the Goddess, or the divine feminine. Early on it was used within matriarchal societies, where the Great Mother God ruled. The Dove symbolism remained because the people still related to the Holy Spirit as a representation of the divine feminine, or the female aspect of God. Never before, through thousands of years of human history, was there a world without the Great Mother. It would take centuries of relentless persecution and slaughter of thousands, and even millions of people by the church clergy and their accomplices to eradicate this idea from the minds of humanity. Ultimately they did not succeed, as the Goddess went underground, and still existed in the collective unconscious, and, therefore, remained a part of Christianity.

Goddess Asherah

The Old Testament preceded the Gospels by five hundred years, and was written at a time of misogynist attitudes among the Jewish men who dominated the women. Before those times, in a society with stronger matriarchal elements, Jewish people worshiped their Mother Goddess, Asherah. In immediately pre-Biblical times, the worship of Asherah was done both in public and in private. The people worshiped the concept of the Mother Creator in her spiritual state; numerous images were created, often as statues, to satisfy the need that people had for tangible visuals of their divinities. At that time, the male consort god Baal already was a part of this divine concept, and often the altars were dedicated to both Asherah and Baal. The idea of the sacred marriage was celebrated: a sacred union of the divine feminine with her masculine counterpart, *hieros gamos*. During the Biblical times, when patriarchy gained control over the lives of women, the concept of the sacred feminine became diluted, weakened by the patriarchal rabbis. Shekinah, as the feminine divine presence on Earth, and Hokhma, as the divine Wisdom, were the archetypes of the former Mother Goddess, but their definitions became nebulous.

Shekinah, Hokhma, and the Holy Spirit

The female gender of God continued to co-exist along the dominant male during Talmudic and Biblical times, and Shekina, Hokhma, and the Holy Spirit overlapped or merged as the female symbols for God. The words themselves have the female gender in Hebrew, and therefore the emphasis on their gender has a more obvious impact than it does in many other languages. Shekinah is perceived as an independent divine entity that is a manifestation of God's presence on earth, and she often argues with the male God in favor of human beings, as the divine intercessor. Hokhma, a concept of the divine female as Wisdom, appears as an intercessor in the Biblical texts, such as the Book of Job, the Book of Proverbs, and later in the Apocrypha. According to Raphael Patai in *Hebrew Goddess,* the Gnostic Hokhma myth originated in Jewish circles; to the Gnostics, she is the *anima mundi*, or the soul of the world.[48] Mary the mother of Jesus and Mary Magdalene are connected to the earlier heritage of the Old Testament as the representatives of the divine feminine within the New Testament.

The chalice, or the sacred vessel, was in pre-Christian times celebrated within the numerous religions of the Great Goddess as the symbol of the Great Mother as the divine woman-creator. Together with many other symbols of the Goddess, it was introduced into early Christianity as a masculine symbol of Christ. However, it retained a great deal of ambiguity regarding its meaning, as the divine feminine connotations persisted, and were incorporated into the legends of the Grail. Today the Holy Grail is often perceived by the people as a sacred object connected to Mary Magdalene.

The perception of Mary Magdalene by the American public is rapidly changing. Today she is seen as not only the female apostle, but also as another face of the divine within the Christian doctrine. As this religion is undergoing a gradual change, it is becoming less misogynist, and more like the original creed initiated by the sacred couple of Jesus and Mary Magdalene that we can glean from the early evidence of the Dead Sea Scrolls, and the Gospels of Mary Magdalene. It is possible, if the emancipation of women continues, that we will end up with a new version of Christianity, which will feel comfortable to women who believe that their spirituality is as important as the one of their male counterparts. I foresee that this transformation of Christianity will happen when the majority of women will feel that way about themselves; it may happen within the next fifty years.

11.

Kyra Belán

9

The Goddesses of Santeria and Voodoo: From Africa and Caribbean

Both Santeria and Voodoo, also spelled Voodou, are religions that were formed and thrive today in the U.S. because of Africa; both entered the North American continent via the Caribbean. They stem from the religions of the Yoruba and Bantu people who were sold as slaves and brought into the new world. Upon their arrival in the early sixteenth century (around 1515), thousands of slaves were immediately indoctrinated into Christianity - baptized and forced to relinquish their own beliefs. Thus, a new syncretic form of the old African religion, in many variations, was formed as the slaves continued to practice their own religion blended with the new. Often, the names of Christian saints were adopted and used to identify the old African deities in order to disguise them and to be able to worship them in secret. This allowed the slaves to keep their true beliefs while outwardly appearing Christian. This strategic maneuver allowed the new religion to first develop in the Caribbean, and then, as the population of African descent was brought as slaves to America, the new syncretic form of the African-Christian cult migrated to the American coastal region and then expanded inland.

It is important to understand that African religions, like the religions of the Native Americans, are earth centered, and have numerous female and male divinities. These religions usually worship one supreme divinity, and the groups of powerful and complex Goddesses and Gods that can be considered as either aspects or children of this Supreme Being. The original creator, which in prehistoric times was perceived in female form, is gynandric; she is the female Mother God, but she is also a male.

When described by the patriarchal scholars, she is usually called a he, and as a result it is mistakenly perceived by the population of western descent in male terms, since these people have been conditioned to worship only a male god, either single or triple. The worshipers in African countries were sophisticated thinkers, and visualized this Supreme Being as an energy or force. They believe that this energy pervades the entire universe, including our planet Earth. Yet, this abstract being is understood as female/male (gynandric or androgynous), since all life in nature is either female or male, although some life forms may change sex during their existences. Also, scientific evidence corroborates the fact that the original gender is female for all, and the male gender develops from the female as a variant. Instinctively or viscerally, the religions of Africa, like those in India or Native Americas, honor the female principle as the central core of all existence.

The belief in a divinity as a part of Nature itself is central within the African culture, and was brought to America. In her book, *Jambalaya*, Luisah Teish explains:

"Prior to the white colonization of the continent West Africans believed in an animated universe, in the process I call "Continuous Creation." Continuous Creation means that the generation and recycling of energy is always in effect.

God is *No Thing*, incomprehensible, and traditionally Africans do not attempt to make images of the Infinite One. God is conceived and spoken of in terms descriptive of creation: the Yoruba say that God is the "Author of Day and Night," "the Discerner of Hearts." The Ngombe of the Congo see God as the "One Who Clears the Forest" and the "One Who Fills Everything." The Akan of Ghana speak of God as the "Ever-Ready Shooter" and the "Killer Mother." The Herrero of Southwest Africa declare that "God has no father and is not a man."

"The Africans realized that whatever we say about God is limited by *our perception* of God; but God is not limited. Everything we know is God, and that which we do not know is also God. God transcends our understanding, and there is nothing beyond or outside of God. Knowable God is the sum total of all the forces of nature in dynamic interaction.

One of our limitations is language, and unfortunately sexist language has insisted on labeling the totality whose intelligence gives birth to us all as a *he*."[49]

Luisah Teish is very aware of how patriarchy has controlled the religions of the world in order to enslave half the population – women, and she feels that it is important that we become conscious of this in order to change our social paradigm in the direction of a more wholesome society. Teish proposes that:

"It is important that gynandry be explored because the oppression of women has been based on an erroneous assumption that the Most High God is a male. We must reverse patriarchal thinking in order to get a balanced perspective.

Knowing that humans formed their concepts of God from the workings of nature, let us turn to creation-in-action, the fetus in the womb. The misogynist view says that the male child is superior to the female. It is a known and accepted medical fact that all fetuses show female physical characteristics first; masculinity is a secondary development. We could, therefore, also say that the prototype for humanity is female."[50]

The spiritual traditions of Africa embraced nature and Mother Earth as an integral part of the universal creator; beneath this universal underlying energy, the worshipers perceive a plethora of divinities known as Orishas or Loas, a second tier of the divine composed of many Goddesses and Gods, sacred ancestors, and numerous nature spirits that are all a part of the sacred continuum. The pantheons of divinities that came to the U.S., Santeria from Cuba and Voodoo of New Orleans from Haiti have many similarities, including the names of the divinities. These religions offer their followers features that seem to satisfy their spiritual quest, the desire to use their extra-sensory perceptions, to attune with nature, and to develop personal power and self-assurance. These beliefs can co-exist with the followers' traditional religions if they so desire. Both Voodoo and Santeria are attractive to women; they stem from the old matriarchal traditions, and women can fully participate as priestesses and practitioners. The divine feminine aspects of these earth-based religions, which have many variations, empower women, add to their self-respect as human beings, and allow them to express themselves as unique individuals. The nature of Voodoo and Santeria beliefs encourages their integration into everyday life of each individual.

Obatala

To the practitioners of Voodoo and Santeria, Obatala is the Supreme Creator. Originally female, she is now androgynous, and came to America via the Caribbean from the Yoruba tradition. She is visualized as a woman dressed in a luminous white dress, with beautiful long pure white hair. She is Wisdom, like Sophia of the Christian Gnostics, possesses infinite power, and is concerned with the affairs of her human children since she shaped them into being. According to the legend, as she subdivided the earthly realms, she gave the sky to the birds, water to the fishes, and the fertile lands to the human beings.

Goddess Oba

The Goddess of the flowing water of rivers, she represents the passage of time and of life. This Goddess has similarities with Saraswati of India. Her powers are great. Oba is invoked by her followers to help them in the matters of dealing with time, and the life giving powers of this water Goddess are invoked to ask for personal life-altering decisions. In times of dry weather, her sacred waters flow to revive the abundance in nature.

Yemaya or Yemaja

Yemaya, also called Yemaja, Yemanja, or Olokun, is the Mother Goddess presiding over the oceans. She is the creator Goddess that is closely related or disguised in Voodoo and Santeria as the Christian Mother of God, the Virgin Mary. Like Mary, Yemaya is particularly important to women and children. She is visualized wearing a long white dress, with a sash of sky blue. Yemaya came from Nigeria and is one of the most important Orishas of Voodoo and of Santeria in America. Yemaya created the Sun, the Moon, the stars, the streams of water, the rivers, and the seas; therefore, she is a major benefactor of humanity. She is also revered for her powers of fertility. The practitioners and priestesses set up her altars in their own homes, although many Marian churches and cathedrals are also considered to be the homes of Yemaya, such as the church of Our Lady of Regla, located in Miami, Florida.

Goddess Oshun

The African Venus/Aphrodite, Oshun, is the Goddess of Love, relationships and divinations; she is visualized as infinitely beautiful. She is known in Haiti as Ersuli. She rules over love, passion, and relationships. She is also a healer, and she taught the Orishas, the priestesses, and the people the arts of divining. This knowledge she gained from Obatala. Oshun is one of the favorite divinities in Santeria and in Voodoo, and is often symbolized by the shells, gold jewelry, and the gold or yellow colors.

Goddess Oya

Oya is of Yoruban origin, and she represents, as the Mother Goddess, the spirit of the rivers including Niger, the waters, the fire, and the winds of change. She is the most feared among the Goddesses as she is in complete control of the fire and the wind. However, she is the creator divinity and supports justice, traditions, and mastery of speech, but also passion and determination. Yoruban women seek her help to gain access to the right words that can lead to the resolution of conflicts and to acquire power. As the Goddess of Transformation she is essential for those who seek change in their lives and is committed to help human beings to go through the necessary steps to achieve their goals.

Both Voodoo and Santeria are syncretic religions and employ Christian symbolism: Mary, Jesus, and the saints are used as equivalents or decoys for the divinities of African origin. These religions, originated by thousands of slaves sold in Africa to be brought into the Caribbean and the Americas, had to remain secret for many years, and secrecy is still a part of the practice. One theory is that after their forceful conversion to Christianity, the slaves re-combined their beliefs, and consequently an amalgamation of the African religion and Christianity was born. Another faction believes that a gradual assimilation of Christianity into African beliefs did not take place; it was a deliberate process. Raul Canizares, author of Cuban Santeria, believes that "the process of aligning Santeria beliefs was less a case of syncretism than of dissimulation – the conscious, deliberate use of elements of Catholicism to allow people to practice their beliefs undisturbed. Building on those findings of other scholars that my training as a *santero* validates as correct, I have devised a model that demonstrates how the dissimulation/deception component functions within the framework of Santería."[51]

Santeria: an Overview of Hierarchical Structure

This religion has developed a complex system of initiations, rituals, and practices usually administered by its priestesses and priests called *santeras* and *santeros*. Even though much more fair to women than the traditional patriarchal religions such as Christianity, Santeria is headed by the highest-ranking male priests called babalaos. However, the *santeras* and *santeros* in America have freed themselves from many of the restrains placed on them, and perform many rituals and services to their congregations or practitioners that were formerly only possible in Cuba if performed by the *babalaos*, thus confirming the fact that the patriarchal prejudice against women in the United States is diminishing.

According to Raul Canizares, the participants of Santeria fall into several distinct categories. One consists of the interested observers, a group that remains outside the religion, but is either curious enough to read and somewhat investigate the practice, or actually conduct research without ever becoming a part of the religion. The next group consists of occasional clients, people who use Santeria for medical reasons, just as if the *santero/santera* were a physician. This group is not very aware of the differences between Santeria and Christianity. However, the next group, which Canizares calls the habitual clients, is aware of the differences between Santeria and Christianity, and uses the services of the *santeros/santeras* frequently. In fact, every move in their lives is done after consulting a practitioner first. Some of these clients are also amulet recipients, which makes them interested and loyal enough to wear an item, usually special beads, that advertise to the general public their involvement in Santería.[52]

The Initiations

All *santeras*, *santeros* and *babalaos* have to go through rigorous training that usually takes three or more years. Each step of the process is completed by going through elaborate initiation rites. Both *santeras* and *santeros* go through the same rituals carefully following a special protocol. The last and most important ritual, to become a *babalao*, takes seven days and is reserved only for the males. This last ritual is supposed to be a secret, however it has been disclosed and written down in Cuba. Now we know that it is about the African roots, and the several African kings, so the *babalao* symbolically becomes a king. There is one known case in America of a woman who was initiated as Ianifa or Mother of the Secrets in 1985, a female equivalent of a babalao. She divulged the information about her initiation, including the photos, to the press believing that the event should be public. The opposition from the American babalaos and santeros was strong, and it is keeping her away from practicing this religion so far. Sexist attitudes within religions are still overwhelming, and the lady, named Patri Dhaifa, remains ostracized, according to Migene Gonzalez-Wippler, author of *Santeria The Religion*, published by Llewellyn in 2007. However, a landmark organization, Universal Sisters, has formed and gathered on May 27th 2011 with the purpose to re-establish women back into religious practices of Santeria and related religions world wide on equal status with men. The meeting took place in Cuba, and is considered a milestone in Santeria, as it is fighting to establish Ianifa title for women practitioners in both Cuba and the U.S.

The rest of the rituals apply equally to both genders. The first one is dedicated to the Orisha Elegua, a male trickster god to whom the initiate pledges allegiance. At this stage the initiates start to understand Santeria as essentially a non-Christian tradition. In the next ceremony, the initiate becomes the warrior, or the *guerrero/guerrera*, and the main Orisha is usually Ogun. At this point the initiate becomes a full-fledged *santero* or *santera* initiate. The initiate receives objects that represent the Orishas. The next ritual has the initiate wear the beads or *collares*, which make it obvious to the world that the person is a part of the Santeria religion.

The step that follows is the *santero/santera* ritual, and at this time one particular Orisha is *seated,* which means that that Orisha possesses the initiate. They can be also called *iyabo,* which means bride, and they are now full practitioners. They learn to perform magic, divination, rituals, and to prepare potions, along with all the other technical or practical aspects of Santeria.

Voodoo

The practice of Voodoo, or Voodou, which developed in New Orleans, is more matriarchal than Santeria, and the women/priestesses are often seen as magical queens of this religion. They are often in charge of the practice, and among them are the most famous and influential Queens of Voodoo, including one of the founding mothers and the best known of all, Marie Laveau. The practitioners are also given more independence, and can make many choices as to which Orisha to pray to and honor. The priestesses and the practitioners, many of which are female, invoke the Seven African Powers. There are seven Orishas: Obatala, Yemaya, Oya, Oshun, Elegua, Chango, and Ogun. But the practitioner can also select her or his helpers from among the enchanted spirits and the ancestors. According to Luisa Teish, *encantados* are thought of as guardian spirits with superhuman powers. They "can predict the future, inspire cooperation from strangers, and help the devotee by granting numerous petitions."[53] The *encantados,* means enchanted spirits in Spanish, and they offer practitioners more opportunities to personalize their individual practices. They select their own saints, and if the results are not satisfactory, the devotees can petition another saint of their choice. The whole operation is strictly between her/him and the saint.

Matriarchal Tradition of Voodoo of New Orleans

Since its inception as a tradition of New Orleans, Voodoo practice has been good to women of all racial backgrounds. It allowed women freedom from slavery or subjugation to men and forged important bonds between women of all classes and races. These bonds improved the existing society. Today, like in the past, Voodoo still functions as a people's religion that does not discriminate against gender or race and is available to those who would like to join regardless of their social positions.

Marie Laveau: The Great Queen of Voodoo

The Voodoo of New Orleans and Louisiana has its origins in Haiti and, in part, Cuba during the eighteenth century. First reference to this religion, derived from Africa, can be found in New Orleans in 1782, when its Spanish governor Galves made an attempt to ban this mystical cult. However, even though there were several important Voodoo Queens before her, the main reason for its existence as a matriarchal repository of knowledge of earth magic, herbal science, and psychic power is due to the fact that Marie Laveau came on the scene as its most brilliant Queen in 1826, embraced this mystical religion and made it popular. Marie Laveau's power was legendary, and she knew that she was in total control of her followers. She called herself the Pope of Voodoo, and she was right. Her contributions to the development of this earth-based religion were considerable, and she is the one largely responsible for the introduction of the Christian Virgin Mary as a major syncretic Goddess of Voodoo, often also representing Yemaya, Oya, Oshun, Erzulie, the Great Mother, or the Great Goddess of Chance. Marie also placed emphasis on the positive magic. This kind of magic lifts the practitioners and helps their lives, their personal growth, and the resolution of their conflicts. It also improves the status of women, the slaves, and the poor by helping them empower themselves. As she accumulated more wealth, her charitable efforts to help the poor increased. Of all the queens or priestesses and the male root doctors or priests of Voodoo, she was probably the most generous to the people.

When Marie Laveau joined Voodoo around 1826 she inherited a problematic and persecuted religion. The practitioners, who first arrived in New Orleans around 1803, were usually from Haiti or sometimes from Cuba and were brought in as slaves. They secretly practiced their rituals in the remote bayous. This included the worship of Orishas or Loas, and of Zombie, a snake that symbolized fertility magic. They danced and played drums, and there was also drinking and lovemaking. The people came to the rituals to gain personal power – acquire a lover, or destroy their enemies, or help their finances or other worldly affairs, or heal their illnesses. The whites were afraid of these gatherings, so they passed a resolution not to allow the Blacks to gather except on Sundays at a place now called the Beauregard Square. Since then, the devotees gathered and continued with their dances while worshiping the African Goddesses and Gods – the Loa or the Orishas, while the whites were appeased by thinking that the rituals were just gibberish. These ceremonies were called the Sunday Congo Dances. At another time, secret rituals were conducted at Lake Pontchartrain.

There were many queens before Marie came along, but she soon became the most powerful and took full control. She added many Christian touches to the rituals taken right from Catholicism, which she also practiced; these include incense, holy water, statues or images of numerous saints and above all, the presence of the Virgin Mary. Some Catholic prayers were also integrated into this new version of Voodoo. Marie was a genius at political strategies and networking, and she invited many important people – usually men – from the white establishment to her events, and started charging fees for them, thus enriching the coffers of Voodoo practice. She gained control of the Congo Square dances by appearing herself and dancing with a large snake in her arms. The wealthy whites flocked to her and paid her to help them manage their lives in everyway, many not able to make a move without her advise, magical spells, or cures. In 1869, Marie Laveau retired at the age of seventy and Marie II, her daughter, took over. She still worked behind the scenes until 1875, and died in 1881 probably at the age of eighty-seven. Her daughter became a very important queen, but she (or any other queen) could not overshadow the grandeur of the mystical and mythical Marie Laveau. Mamzelle Marie Laveau's grave in New Orleans is a sacred shrine to the Voodoo practitioners. Offerings are made to this important altar, and xs are scribbled over the stone surface for good luck. The procession of visitors to her gravesite is constant, since the religion of Voodoo, in spite of some negative press, continues to flourish. Luisa Teish, author of *Jambalaya* and a priestess dedicated to Oshun in the Lucimi tradition, underscores the importance of the presence of Mary within the religion:

"The slaves saw in Mary, Star of the Sea, their own Ocean Goddess Yemonja, and they embraced Her. They drew parallels between the saints and their own deities in order to worship them with impunity.

But the African way was and is the way of power. So Mary not only represented Yemonja but was also recognized as *another power*, a sister, another Goddess who could be invoked to work magic on behalf of the slaves.

The integrative power of adaptation created Macumba and Candomble in Brazil, Lucimi or Santeria in Cuba, Santeria in Puerto Rico, Voudou or Hoodoo in Haiti and New Orleans."[54]

Both the Voodoo and Santeria are flourishing today in America. Services are offered, and numerous shops sell the ingredients necessary for the spells and herbal medicine, as well as numerous objects, such as the statuary of the saints. The internet provides additional access to the regular or prospective practitioners all over the country. Although there is no statistical information regarding the adepts because of the secrecy of these religions, the presence of the businesses related to these beliefs attests that the populations of both are steadily increasing. These faiths fulfill the needs of certain portions of the population better than any other available religion, and they have millions of adepts. It is probable that in the near future these figures will be available to the public, as more people will feel entitled to practice their non-traditional faiths openly.

Kyra Belán

12.

Kyra Belán

10

The Goddess of Wicca and Paganism: The Legacy of Matriarchal Europe

Wicca was brought to America from Europe, as the settlers of western European descent arrived in waves after the "discovery" of the Americas. It is probably the oldest religion of the world that has continued into our historical time without interruptions, but not without intense oppression. The legends and myths of this religion, also called Witchcraft, may date as far back as 35,000 years. This chronology places Wiccan origins at a time when social structures were matriarchal, ruled by the Great Mother Goddess as their dominant divinity. The religion of Wicca appeals to contemporary minds because of its flexibility: the worshipers can still maintain their place, if they wish, at their conventional church, or choose to solely immerse themselves in Wiccan philosophy. Wicca devotees and the Pagans have much in common, and the terms are often used interchangeably; both worship female and male divine principles and deeply love Mother Earth. There is also much in common between the Native American beliefs and Wicca: both believe in nature spirits as sacred, and venerate Mother Nature, and its animal beings. The ancient religion of Wicca has understood the rhythms and the cyclical nature of the physical existence in time. It is profound enough to comprehend that both earthly and heavenly realms are imbued with the same energy that is divine on every level, and that you cannot have a true understanding of divinity by excluding the female principle, which is largely absent within the dominant patriarchal religions. The totality of the universe, they feel, has to be represented by the divine source. They visualize it as the triple goddess or female trinity: the Goddess as Creator, the Nurturing Mother

Goddess, and the Wise Goddess. The triple deity represents the cycles of nature: the birth, the mature existence, and the transformative years that culminate with death and then the cycle repeats itself. The Wiccan practitioners usually believe in reincarnation, as this belief was espoused by the old European cultures from which this religion originated. In fact, the belief in reincarnation was nearly universal in the ancient world. The Wiccan male principle is expressed through a male god-warrior, who originated as the son/consort of the Great Goddess.

The followers od Wicca have a multitude of Goddesses, or names for their Mother Goddess available to them through the Old European heritage starting with the remote Goddesses of prehistory. The prehistoric Great Mother was the Goddess of the Animals, and as such was often worshiped in caves, where her beasts were depicted, often as running in groups, often in profile; however, sometimes the artists used foreshortening, depicting the animal body in perspective.

To the prehistoric minds, the realm of the Great Mother encircled the entire universe, which also included the skies. She was the original Sun Goddess, Moon Goddess, and Star Goddess, the Creator, All That Is. As the time elapsed and the new male god became important, she started to share her Sun Goddess powers with him; later he took over as the Sun God in many myths. Through times, she kept her Moon Goddess aspect, which is still revered today as one of her important cyclical attributes among the Wiccan and Pagan worshipers. The Moon Goddess aspect of the Mother is clearly depicted in the famous pre-historic Venus of Laussel (circa 20,000 B C E) a relief sculpture of old Europe where the Mother is depicted holding a cow horn, symbolizing the crescent; thirteen incised lines can be seen on it, a representation of thirteen lunar months. The main celebrations of the Great Mother took place during the solstices and equinoxes. The priestesses honored the Mother and her newborn child, and, with the help of the community, circular structures or henges were constructed, inside which the ceremonies were held. Each year was visualized as a circle divided in eight solar and lunar rituals; a spiral progression of time was gleaned from this obvious circularity. The beginnings of astronomy and sciences were formed, and the priestesses, in their contemplation of natural phenomena, were able to delve deep into the mysteries of the universe. But perhaps the most important part of this religion was the development of the healing powers of herbal medicine by the priestesses: their ability to cure and transform people's lives was irreplaceable. They also developed white or beneficial magic for the benefit of the devotees.

Even during the old European patriarchal systems, after the warrior-kings from the east defeated the Goddess-centered civilizations, matriarchal elements were still a part of the ancient culture, and the Great Mother's powers were distributed among numerous goddesses and gods. Often she also became the wife of the new dominant male god, who was formerly her son. As the new patriarchies strengthened, her official powers gradually diminished. Yet the Wicca, even after it became an occult religion during the Inquisition, continued to worship the Goddess as their dominant divine figure. The practitioners did not confine themselves just to the goddesses of old Europe, but also worshipped many ancient Egyptian divinities, particularly the Great Goddess Isis. Today in America most participants of the Wicca or The Craft do not like to be in the limelight, and many still worship in secret, or as solitary practitioners. Yet there is a loosely connected network of Wicca and Paganism that spans the entire country, and there is a degree of communication between the adepts either through the internet, the New Age bookstore events, or the gatherings that at times become quite public, like the events that are scheduled at the Nashville Parthenon, a symbolic temple of the Goddess Athena.

The loosely connected country-wide network of the Wiccan or Witchcraft adepts is generally grass roots based and operated. The practitioners gather in covens, small groups of a few people, with a maximum number of thirteen members. To be a part of the coven, the adept must go through a lengthy training, which may take months or years, and at least three initiations. There are many more applicants than covens, and therefore there are also many solitary practitioners, some of which eventually develop their own covens. Occasionally, a coven may expand over the allowed number, and then it is called a grove. Each group may develop unique variations of rituals and ceremonies, but in essence they have certain characteristics that are common to all, which I will attempt to summarize here. What appears to be central to all the practice is the desire of the practitioners to develop their inner connection with the divine source through understanding the subtle and unseen energies that flow through the physical and psychic universes, and to access the realm of deep consciousness that is also permeated with these divine forces. The devotees learn how to improve themselves by practicing Magic. The rituals of the Craft are designed to awaken the hidden and undeveloped potentials that individuals have in order to better understand and streamline the source, or the unseen benevolent forces of the universe, or the psychophysical world in favor of an individual, but without repercussions to the rest of the world. Since the famous saying of the Craft is *what you send, returns three times over*, the people of the Craft are fearful to make a mistake that would injure or produce a set-back for anyone in the world, as they believe that this error would injure them even worse. Therefore, the sense of justice is very strong in the practitioners of Wicca, and a sense of fairness pervades their rituals and acts of Magic.

In Witchcraft or Wicca the *circle*, as a shape, has a prominent significance: this perfect geometric form, symbolic of the Goddess and Mother Earth, is used in the rituals of Magic that often have a healing purpose. Casting the circle is an important part of the magic process, and all rituals take place within this magic circle, or the circle of life. This establishes the territory that represents a temple, whether an indoor one, such as the living room of the person of the Craft, an outdoor space, or a part of the wilderness, which is sacred since all of Mother Nature is. The practitioners of Wicca celebrate and invoke their mystical elements, which to them are four: earth, fire, air, and water. Starhawk, a renown author and priestess of the craft, talks about them in her book, *The Earth Path*: "While we know that air, fire, water, and earth are not elements in the same way as hydrogen, oxygen, nitrogen, and carbon are, they each represent great cyclical processes of transformation that sustain life. The whirling cauldron of the atmosphere, the energy exchanges fueled by the sun, the cyclical journey of water from raindrop to stream to ocean to raindrop, the endogenic cycle of rock formation and plate tectonics, and the cycles of birth, growth, decay, and regeneration are some of the most basic processes of Gaia's philosophy.[55]

Wicca is a joyous religion or practice; the rituals, like those of Voodoo and the Native American Earth-centered religions, are performed with chanting, dancing, drumming, and instrumental music. Some of the traditional chants are quite old, possibly dating back to the old matriarchal Goddess rituals. The divinities invoked vary and could be a specific Goddess or God, or several, depending on the needs of the particular coven. The raising of the *cone of spiritual power* involves, like many other rituals, the visualization process. Sometimes, like in other religions that we have already discussed, a person or several people may fall into a trance, a physical-spiritual state that is produced by altered consciousness.

To explain the premises of the Craft, Starhawk declares in her book titled *The Spiral Dance*, her philosophy about Wicca that rings true with other practitioners:

"Mother Goddess is reawakening, and we can begin to recover our primal birthright, the sheer, intoxicating joy of being alive. We can open new eyes, and we can see that there is nothing to be saved *from*, no struggle of life *against* the universe, no God in the outside world to be feared and obeyed; only the Goddess, the Mother, the turning spiral that whirls us in and out of existence, whose winking eye is in the pulse of being -- birth, death, rebirth -- whose laughter courses through all things and who is found only through love: love of trees, of stones, of sky and clouds, of scented blossoms and thundering waves, of all that runs and flies and swims and crawls on her face; through love of ourselves; life-dissolving world-creating orgasmic love of each other; each of us unique and natural as a snowflake, each of us our own star, her Child, her lover, her beloved, her Self."[56]

Like the circle and the spiral, the *triangle* has a very important significance within the Wicca. The shape, a symbol for the feminine divine, has come down to us from prehistoric times. Within the contemporary traditions of American Wicca, the triangle is a symbol for the three aspects of the divine as it relates to human beings. The top is symbolic of the Holy Spirit, the abstract universal energy or All That Is. The left corner, from the point of view of the observer facing it, is the Goddess, the divine female energy, and the right corner is symbolic of the God, or the male divine energy. Some covens pay more attention to the symbolism of the triangle than others.

The Wiccan practitioners regard as of utmost importance another symbol: the pentagram or a five-pointed star. This symbol can be traced to European tradition from around the twelfth century, but it is probably much older. It has many meanings, such as the four directions of the universe and the Divine, or the Spirit, or the Goddess. It can also signify the four directions and the human being. When enclosed in a circle, it is called a pentacle, and as such is often worn by the adepts on a chain around their necks. Its enemies have maligned this Wiccan symbol; they try to associate it with the Christian devil, an entity in which the Wiccans do not believe. Hollywood movies picked up on this sensationalism and made the association even stronger. The practitioners of Wicca still are victims of this association today, and because of this, many are still reluctant to disclose their practice, although others openly practice the Craft.

Wicca is a religion that has accumulated a large collection of poems, songs, prayers, and rituals. The adepts also have numerous books for studies in groups or covens or as solitary witches. One of the most interesting books that have a long tradition of existence is *A Witches' Bible*. Perhaps Janet and Steward Ferrar wrote the most popular version of this book. It contains the famous *Charge of the Goddess*. This *Charge* was rewritten in the fifties by the famous witch and writer Doreen Valiente, and in the seventies by Starhawk, and it clearly places Wicca as one of the most joyous and positive religions of the world. At the same time, the Wiccan philosophy is extremely pure in terms of ethical behavior of each individual involved in the Craft, who is bound to strict rules not to harm her/himself or any other individual or living entity, and to respect the environment. The commitment of this religion to the purity of each individual, her/his psychic development in a positive direction, and its concern and love of the environment or Mother Earth seems to draw many contemporary thinkers into the Craft. The positive philosophy of Wicca is constantly attracting new practitioners, and this religion's popularity is on the increase in America.

The religion of Wicca or Craft is a form of Paganism that espouses a philosophy of life that is totally different from that of the dominant patriarchal religions such as Christianity. At this time of ecological crisis, it is particularly important to recognize that the fundamental premise of Wicca is that the divine essence pervades both the heavenly and the earthly realms, and that nature and all living things have to be respected and cherished, as they are all components of physical existence that is divine, perfect, and must be respected. This point of view at a time when we must change our destructive habits to stop global warming and reverse the damage already perpetrated upon our planet is refreshing and beneficial; people who think along these lines are the ones that will help restore the Earth to its previous state of wholeness. On the contrary, the Christian philosophy, adhered to for the last two thousand years, has established many destructive habits, such as the use of fuel, the destruction of the tropical forests, the extinction of animal species, and the industrialization of crop production. Above all, the belief in the dualism of humans and nature – particularly of men versus nature – has been entrenched far too long in the human psyche, and the structure of the government. Beyond that, the belief that humans – or more precisely men – are entitled to explore and destroy nature, which was created by a male patriarchal god at their service, is embedded within the western Christian culture. Therefore, the fact that Christianity managed to destroy Paganism in Europe and then the Native American religions of the new world has led us, as the humanity and the Americans, to the state of affairs we are now immersed in and have to correct. The beneficial point of view of the Wicca movement, like that of the Native Americans, is to respect, restore, and above all, love our Mother Earth.

Hollywood movie productions have been regularly depicting the witches and Pagan or Wicca worshipers as the followers of the devil. This negative commercialism stems from the desire to sell their films, and therefore much of the output caters to the viewers who look for a thriller. Contrary to Hollywood's depictions of Wicca as a devil worshipping and gloomy religion, the followers do not worship the devil; the latter is a part of Christian beliefs, but is not necessarily encountered within other religions. On the contrary, love, joy, magic, and healing are the founding cornerstones or principles of Wicca. It is a challenge for the participants to maintain positive, joyous, and loving attitude, while gaining spiritual control over their personal reality, and they are committed to developing themselves throughout their lives. Therefore, many rituals provide the necessary support for this direction in the lives of the practitioners, and they can be simple, elegant, or elaborate, and can vary according to each solitary follower or coven's inclinations.

The Magic of Healing is very important to the members of Wicca, and many rituals have also been developed to increase or promote healing. Perhaps that is the reason why Goddess Isis, described in chapter four of this book, resonates strongly within the believers of the Craft. This creator Goddess, a Great Magician and Healer, as well as a Savior to her believers, is dear to the hearts of the Wiccan population in America. Rituals to celebrate, evoke, and pray to Goddess Isis are an important part of the culture of the Craft. The presence of this Goddess is felt in many ways by the practitioners, and her statues, images, and symbols, including the Egyptian cross known as the ankh, are available for purchase at the specialty book and gift stores that cater to this sector of the population. However, the devotees of Wicca see all the thousands of Goddesses that have been worshipped in the past or present as the faces of the Creator Mother God. Therefore, there are infinite variations of the Lady, who has so many names, appearances, symbols, and attributes, based on the mythologies that came down to us from every corner of the world.

It is obvious that Wicca is a female-friendly religion. While most dominant religions are patriarchal and worship male God or Gods, Wicca places emphasis on the female aspect of God. The position of a woman within the religious hierarchy is equal to that of a man, if not superior. Some forms of Wicca worship only the divine feminine; the best known of these is the Dianic form of Wicca, founded by Z. Budapest, who is its foremost priestess and author of several books. The Dianic Wicca members must be female, and only the Goddess is worshiped. The favorite Goddess of these Wiccans is Diana, originally worshiped by the ancient Romans as the Creator Mother God, but her role was later diminished by the patriarchal take over of Greece and Rome during ancient times, and she is known within patriarchal societies as the Virgin Goddess of Nature and the animals. A religion that worships the Goddess instead of the familiar male God of the male-centered cultures fulfills the need to bring some balance to a civilization that overemphasizes the masculine over the feminine, rendering a culture too much in favor of one gender over the other.

Goddess Diana or Artemis

Diana to the ancient Romans and Artemis to the ancient Greeks, she was the triple Goddess: the Virgin and Moon Goddess that awakens and creates nature, the Mother of all living beings, and the Huntress or Destroyer and Transformer of life in death. The old religion of Diana was wide spread through the entire ancient world. During early Christianity, it presented a serious threat to the new patriarchal religion, and the church fathers often equated her with the Virgin Mary. Numerous ancient sites such as wooded groves were consecrated to her, as well as many beautiful temples. She was considered the protector of the animals, and her spirit was said to fill the trees. One of the most famous temples dedicated to Diana/Artemis was located in Ephesus. During early Christianity this temple was re-dedicated to the Virgin Mary, and a legend was created that claimed that Mary spend her days after the death of Christ there. Her tomb also was believed to be located in Ephesus. In her book, *The Woman's Encyclopedia of Myths and Secrets*, Barbara G. Walker mentions, "Some Christians even remembered that Diana was the triple deity that ruled the world. A

14-century poem attributed to the Bishop of Meaux said Diana was an old name for the Trinity."[57]

Paganism

The religion of Wicca is a form of Paganism, but there are differences between the two. The Pagan worshippers are generally less formal regarding their rituals and are more loosely organized. The adepts of Paganism, also called Neo-Paganism, like Wicca, often trace themselves back to their roots – the many ancient religions that worshiped the Great Mother Goddess, and later numerous Goddesses and Gods. They have many choices of divinities to emulate, but all share their love for nature, ignore the Christian duality that places Mother Earth in a precarious situation of exploitation, and honor both female and male divinities. There are many versions of Paganism, but typically the covens are loosely put together and the practitioners subscribe to a variety of rituals and believe in more that one divinity, and at times they include not only the goddesses and gods of Europe, but also of other continents. The Pagans seem to resent too much structure and authority within their groups since each individual is considered unique and free to make many decisions within the flexible parameters of their religion.

Paganism, like other ancient religions, has continued to be a part of American culture through myths, metaphors, and numerous visual symbols firmly ingrained in the psyche of the citizens of this nation. In particular, female divinities have been a part of the visual culture through the arts, and often the public monuments. The Goddess Columbia, originally a Roman divinity, and a form of the Goddess of Liberty, symbolically dominates our nation's capital, Washington in the District of Columbia. Her statue is located on top of the dome of the building of Congress. The nation's capital houses so many statues of the goddesses that it has been called the city of the Goddess. Numerous pagan goddesses adorn other major American cities, fulfilling the role of the female divine symbols, usually absent from the male dominated patriarchal religions. These images are a part of human subconscious, which craves them to fill the void left by patriarchy. The female creative-generative force within the half the population of this country, unable to legitimately manifest itself through the establishment, thrives as an undercurrent within the masculine culture, often taking powerful, mythical manifestations. Those persons who are consciously involved in paganism often keep their practices secret, not unlike the secret societies, such as masonic orders.

Whether Wiccan or Pagan, the followers of these religions are people eager to improve their lives; they believe in an innate right to happiness, and passionately love Mother Nature and Mother Earth. They enjoy a religious system that allows them to express themselves as individuals, and manage their own beliefs. Women have equal rights and power within their religious hierarchy; this is unusual within the dominant patriarchal faiths. The above qualities make Wicca and Paganism very desirable to many, and in spite of the resistance from the patriarchal cultural establishment, both branches are constantly growing and evolving. It is logical to assume that this interest in women friendly religions will continue to increase.

Kyra Belán

13.

Afterword
Spirituality in the New Millennium

American society has undergone major changes since the nineteen-sixties. Old religious philosophies are no longer relevant to people who are educated, open to multiculturalism, and have access to an unlimited amount of information through the internet and mass media. They are concerned about the reality of increasing population, consumerism, economic problems, and global warming. Possibly the greatest impact on the religious-philosophical thinking of today is the fact that women have become aware of their value as individuals living in a world that hopes to create equal opportunities for all. Women are no longer willing to accept the restrictions placed by the old patriarchal religions on their personal freedoms and condone their second-class status as individuals. The controls established for women within the existing andro-centric religions have shackled them with prescribed roles that always favor the male gender. This history of female oppression and slavery still has a hold on women even within the U.S. today. However, the majority of women have broken free, and they are a formidable force behind the constant changes that are going on within the various spiritual movements of this millennium.

The patriarchal establishment of male privilege is holding on to its old beliefs, but its grip on women is slipping away. Through the ages, supporters of the old views staged organized backlashes against women during the times when the shackles on women's minds and bodies seemed to loosen up. Their tactics varied, but the best known repercussions against the feminization of Christianity a few centuries ago were the infamous and vicious witch burnings in Europe and the disgraceful Salem Witch hunts, trials, tortures, and killings in America. Sometimes dismissed by the patriarchal system as the hallucinations of a few, these organized attacks on women have slowed down the progress of past generations of women who were fighting to recover their human rights and their religious freedoms. Patriarchal religions have been used for many centuries to control women and to keep them in place, thus retaining the status quo of the dominator social order. However, we have reached the point in our society that shows the need for an expansion, modification, and ultimately a major change within the patriarchal religious philosophies.

American women are in the forefront of this change; however, many American men are also unhappy with the limitations of the official religious doctrines. Both genders desire more flexibility for their beliefs and are ready to experiment with their religious philosophies. The public desires a new religion that is less restrictive, more positive, and is in tune with their physical, spiritual, and psychological experiences. As the physical world around us has become better understood and the existence of the inner world of each individual has expanded by conscious efforts on the part of each individual, the desire for a deeper, personal, yet sensible religion has become apparent. Currently, people are seeking inspiration for their beliefs from many sources. It is clear that these sources usually provide the missing feature of the dominant patriarchal beliefs: the presence of the divine feminine. To fill the missing void of the Mother God archetype, the seekers look for it in the beliefs of other cultures, or the ancient and prehistoric past. These religions manifest for the believer not only the usual God the Father, but also the absent God the Mother. The recovered divine feminine aspect of God is perceived as loving, compassionate, nurturing, understanding, and forgiving. The Mother Creator is back, manifesting Herself in many forms.

What is happening to the Christian religion today is the re-examination and re-interpretation of the New Testament and the Old Testament, and this examination of the old texts will continue. As a result, the future of Christianity as a patriarchal religion headed by an all-male trinity may be limited. The new emerging Christianity will become a religion for those who still crave tradition, but demand the re-insertion of the divine feminine. For many people who have been reading about the earlier, more inclusive forms of their religion, it already has. Another radical amendment to traditional Christian doctrine will attenuate or eliminate the dichotomy that has been so damaging for the environment and the animals – the idea that everything earthly is inferior to everything spiritual. This process has begun to take root and will continue to evolve. Eventually two other patriarchal strongholds – Judaism and Islam – will recognize the divine feminine that existed in times which preceded these religions on their own soil in the middle east. These adjustments will benefit not just America, but the entire planet.

In order to maintain a peaceful co-existence, the inclusion of female spirituality into the dominant male-centered religions of the world is critical, and America is leading the way in that direction. Women are the natural peacemakers, and are already contributing to the peace maintenance processes of the world, even though their inclusion into the power systems of the governments and the military is not equal to men's. Even in America, the amount of people that get elected to senate and congress are heavily skewed toward the male gender, and so far we have not elected a woman president or vice president. This inequality in the government is also due to the fact that the equal right for women have not been ratified or passed, and the fact that women get paid less than men also corroborates this lack of equality for women in all areas of life. Raised as second class citizens, the girls of the country do not have their history fairly represented in the textbooks, and their school curriculum clearly favors the male privilege, as their being raised, many falling into the subservient positions, accepting them as a given, as barriers to their gender. Violence against women continues, as well as female sexual trafficking, and sexual slavery of women and female children. Obviously, women have a long way to go, and the adjustments within the religious dogma will contribute to the improvement of the mind set of the female children; they will be ready to accept their roles in our society as equals more freely, after these adjustments have been made for the inclusion of women into the mainstream religions.

The religions of the new millennium are transforming themselves by including the divine feminine for another important reason: the preservation of the planet. With the inclusion of the feminine face of God as a legitimate aspect of human culture, the concept of the universality of the divine that includes both the physical and the spiritual worlds will replace the old divisive philosophy. The spiritual unity between the earthly and the heavenly realms has been always understood by those cultures, past or present, that include the divine feminine into their religious cosmologies alongside with the masculine. The social structures of the prehistoric and ancient cultures of old Europe and the Americas were either matriarchal or had strong matriarchal roots. Their religions were inclusive and celebrated the divine feminine. The concept of Mother Earth as sacred was omnipresent within these beliefs.

As we are experiencing global warming, the decimation of the rain forests, the extinction of numerous plant and animal species, and the deterioration of our planet due to the toxic nature of current technologies, we are depriving our future generations of natural resources that are available to us today. The mindset that drives these technologies has to be changed, but in order for this to happen, the old patriarchal dichotomy of earthly-as-bad and heavenly-as-good has to be eradicated. This change can only take place with the help of benevolent religions that support the new mindset. Science alone cannot effect this change of mindset. However, this change has already taken place within the scientific minds that lead the research, which is enabling us to develop Earth-friendly technologies. James Lovelock and Lynn Margolis initially formulated the new scientific construct, known as the Gaia Theory, and it currently dominates scientific establishment. This theory recognizes that our planet Earth is a living organism and, traveling through space, it carries the rest of the living organisms on or within its surface. We, the human beings, are utterly dependent on the planet that generates everything that exists: the totality of nature. Mother Earth is our one and only home. Acclaimed scientist James Lovelock explains: "This theory sees the evolution of the material environment and the evolution of organisms as tightly coupled into a single and indivisible process or domain."[58] According to Lovelock all the organisms are collections of living beings. Human beings are collections of organs, which can exist independently if properly nourished, and these organs are composed of cells that used to exist independently from each other. Therefore, "the cells themselves, as Lynn Margolis has shown, are communities of microorganisms that once lived free."[59]

Gaia, the planet, is the ultimate collector of living beings that totally depend on her for their survival. The Gaia theory is the subject of a book by a brilliant scientist Elizabeth Sahtouris who is known to research across disciplines such as philosophy, biology, geology, and atmospheric science. In her provocative book, titled *Gaia The Human Journey From Chaos to Cosmos*, Sahtouris explains our planet Earth, Gaia, as a living organism that accommodates all life, including human beings, as life within life. The ancient Greeks and other ancient, as well as some contemporary non-mainstream cultures such as the Native Americans, understood this long ago. The typical pre-patriarchal creation myths often had the Goddess emerge from the primordial void, and create Earth from herself; this creation act included nature, animals, and human beings. Elizabeth Sahtouris describes the ancient Greek creation myth as follows:

"The story of Gaia's dance begins with an image of swirling mist in the black nothingness called Chaos by the ancient Greeks — an image reminding us of modern photos of galaxies swirling in space. In the Myth it is the dancing goddess Gaia, swathed in white veils as she whirls through the darkness. As she becomes visible, and her dance grows ever more lively, her body forms itself into mountains and valleys; then sweat pours from her to pool into seas, and finally her flying arms stir up a wind-sky she calls Ouranus – still the Greek word for sky – which she wraps around herself as protector and mate."[60]

Then Goddess Gaia proceeds with the creation of nature, animals, and the first set of goddesses and gods called the Titans. Then the Titans pro-created and, as a result, the second generation of divinities, the Olympian goddesses and gods appeared. The Titans ended up creating the human beings. The primal Goddess Gaia cares for all her children and regularly allows her wisdom to leak through the layers of the Earth onto a series of sacred locations on the surface. Such sites as Delphi, where the priestesses disseminated Gaia's advise to the mortals, were considered particularly mystical. The knowledge about our planet Gaia is still available to all of us, if we care to gather it like the scientists and creative individuals do through time. But we, for the last two thousand years, have denied the importance of our planet, and some extreme male-centered religions still do. Although Christianity has softened its stance on the evils of the physical world as opposed to the perfection of the spiritual one, the duality - earthly/bad, and heavenly/good - is still a part of its doctrine that is loaded with strongly masculine connotations built into its philosophy. Due to the critical situation we are in, as our planet is being depleted, there is no choice: we have to start loving and respecting Mother Earth. It is an issue of our own survival as a species. Our religious beliefs need to be adjusted to resonate with the facts of our science and with our psycho-philosophical evolution.

Christianity, the dominant religion of the Americas, has adopted numerous symbols and rituals that, for many thousands of years, originally were created by and used by the female oriented religions of the past. The cross is usually considered a Christian symbol of prime importance; in the ancient world of Europe and Africa the cross was used as a symbol by the Goddess centered and Pagan religions. The Egyptian version, the ankh, is particularly well known today; it has a looped top, symbolizing the vaginal opening, while the bottom part of the cross is symbolic of male genitals. Egyptian Goddess Isis is frequently represented holding the ankh. The dying and resurrecting gods of numerous Pagan religions were symbolized by the cross, and were often represented holding it. In Celtic matriarchal religions, the cross and the circle in the middle represented both the male and female genitalia, and the union of the divine feminine and masculine, or *Hieros Gamos*. In Christianity the cross was "not shown in Christian art until six centuries after Christ."[61] It was introduced as a symbol during the sixth century. The divine trinity, another symbol of the sacred, was originally all female representing the three aspects of the Mother God: the Virgin, the Mother, and the Wise Woman. It was transformed during Christianity into an all-male trinity. Within the Pagan and matriarchal religions the body of a woman, as the creator of beings, was believed to be sacred and was represented by a chalice. However, during Christianity a disembodied male god replaced a woman-goddess, with her life giving abilities; this type of reasoning would seem unnatural to the ancient people. The chalice, a symbol of the Goddess, became another male symbol, an allusion to the blood of Christ.

Attributes of the Great Goddess, such as her life-giving womb and her nurturing milk were celebrated by the religions of the past for thousands of years. The belief that the heavenly body of the Goddess that produced the Sun, the Moon, and the stars also created the Milky Way appeared in many myths. Within these belief systems it was natural to celebrate the unique creative feminine force, a Mother God that was also the Great Nurturer, our Mother Earth. The women and female animals were celebrated and respected for their innate gifts to birth and nurture the beings that inhabited the planet. Christian fathers took these honors away from women by proclaiming female sexuality as sinful, an act that culminated in persecution of them as witches. Innumerable women died after torture, often burned alive under this misogynist religion governed by the celibate male priesthood. Bright thinkers, including nineteenth century artist William Blake, knew that there was a connection between the patriarchal religion and the institutionalization of women as sex slaves in the brothels; this is also true about the contemporary sex slave trade business. Today, in countries driven by patriarchal religions, sex trafficking of women and female children is a very big business, third in profits behind war and illegal drug businesses.

There is a solid connection between a social structure of a culture and a religion of that culture. In spite of all the progress made in America we still have pockets of patriarchal religious extremism. The Mormon Polygamist cult, a religion derived from Christianity that believes that Jesus was a polygamous Messiah, promotes rape of female children in this country. Not currently connected with the official Mormon religion, the polygamists are living in secret compounds in Texas, Arizona, and Utah. They are older men – usually much older – who force the female children into "marrying" them and convince them that the male God condones this practice that results in their rapes and multiple pregnancies. These underage uneducated mothers are kept isolated from society; the powerful older males - pedophiles - keep them dependent for their basic needs of life such as food and shelter. Often, these underage mothers are not able to escape their abusers.

Largely due to the fact that in America people have better access to education and cyber-culture, people are more aware of their past history, and its current richness and complexity. Women are emerging as a force that effects change in the areas of conservation of the environment, peace keeping, equal treatment of genders and races, animal protection, and, above all, the gradual acceptance of the divine feminine within the dominant male-centered religions. This movement, although present all over the world, is spearheaded by the American women. Indeed women are very interested in Marian apparitions, miracles, healings, and messages that abound all over the world. Marian events of all sorts occur with uncanny regularity in America and all over the planet. In the eighties, a particular abundance of apparitions of the Virgin Mary took place in a small village of Mejugorje, beginning on June 24, 1981 and ending in 1988. This event was fully supported by women and men from the U. S.; thousands made pilgrimages to the area located in what then was a small village in central Yugoslavia. Like with many other visitations by the Virgin Mary, major interest in this event was fueled by the numerous miraculous healings, thousands of which have been documented. Although patriarchal Christianity is never too happy to approve these miracles as genuine, and the church fathers rarely mention the Christian Mother of God during their sermons, regular people bypass that technicality and visit the sites of the apparitions by the thousands in search of health and other benefits that may result from the contact with the divine feminine. While these apparitions take place frequently in America, it is in Mexico where the temples dedicated to the Virgin Mary were built with the approval from Catholic Church and where the most important Marian relic, the *tilma*, is located. That site, dedicated to Guadalupe or the Dark Madonna, although famous for its extensive pilgrimages, is not utilized enough to celebrate the divine feminine by the Christian establishment. It will probably take decades for the celibate all-male leadership of this religion to warm up to women, but as the power of the female gender increases, it will eventually take place.

Marian apparitions, more often than not to women, take place across the U.S. in both large and small towns. The events happen frequently and do not always attract the news media. The miraculous healings usually occur, and The Virgin Mary addresses the pilgrims as her children, reminding them that She is their protective loving Mother. Since Mary is the sacred feminine being that is best known among the established religions, people tend to relate to any manifestation of the divine in female form as the presence of Mary, the Mother of Christian God. Therefore it is very likely that, distorted through human senses, any time the essence of God the Mother manifests on this Earth, most people believe that the divine apparition must be from a religion that they are familiar with, usually Christianity. When perceiving the apparitions, whether visual or internal voices or images, the receiving person or medium has to interpret the events through the use of the language. The words have their limitations, and in a patriarchal society sexist language often dominates; it is usually the only tool of expression available to the recipient of the spiritual event. The limitations of a language can modify or transform the message to a large degree. The particular mindset of an individual receiving the spiritual message also affects the perception and the translation of that message.

One of the many Marian appearances in the state of Florida takes place once a month in the city of Hollywood. Rosa Lopez, a local resident, believes that she is the recipient of monthly visitations by The Virgin Mary in her own house located in a modest middle class community. She is the only one that is able to see, hear, and feel the apparitions of Mary, and is also believed to be able to transmit this divine energy to others in a form of miraculous healings. For the last fourteen years her yard, and later her entire house has been open to the endless visits of the pilgrims; they are usually Hispanic, but also may be Caucasian, Asian, Afro-Hispanic, or African American. During these visitations many people who looked up to the sky have seen the Sun gyrate and the clouds form anthropomorphic figures that resembled the Virgin Mary or the face of Mary, the face of Jesus, or angelic beings. The portals, or illuminated openings in the sky also appeared on the photographs taken by the visitors. Some of these photographs showed an uncanny resemblance to these subjects, while others only vaguely resembled them. The press and the local television stations reported these events from time to time, but often they were simply ignored. The Vatican, usually skeptical regarding most miraculous apparitions of the Virgin, does not officially acknowledge or sanction this site or its events. However, the ecclesiastic authorities do not desire to prevent the pilgrims from attending.

On a sunlit morning during the month of June, my husband and I drove over to pay a visit to Rosa at her house. At the entrance, near a large statue of crucified Christ and a smaller one of a standing Virgin Mary, visitors were walking by or sitting on the conveniently located garden benches. A volunteer directed us inside the house, replete with the images of Mary and her Son, and we found ourselves in front of a makeshift altar. The visitors were lighting the candles or writing their wishes and requests on small pieces of paper and placing them in one of the two baskets located under the altar. Together with the rest of the pilgrims, we were directed to a hallway that exited into the back yard, where many white plastic chairs were placed around a white plaster statue of Mary wearing a crown of live flowers. Several trees and plants in this garden created a pleasant ambiance, conducive to relaxation or meditation. When everyone was seated, Rosa, dressed in a modest long dress, entered the yard together with several of her male and female volunteers. They got seated among us in a central location near the statue of Mary. For about fifty minutes, Rosa and her volunteers, including a girl in her early teens, were chanting prayers. They were dedicated to Mary, Jesus, or God the Father. It was obvious that for most visitors this was a trance inducing experience; people looked increasingly relaxed, and many had their eyes closed in deep meditation. Rosa, a plump and matronly lady of mid years with a pleasant smile, announced that she had just come back from her trip to Ecuador, and let us know that a site was donated there for the building of a new sanctuary dedicated to The Virgin Mary. Shortly after, she seemed to fall into a deep trance; then she spoke out the messages that she was receiving from the Mother of God. She spoke in Spanish, but the messages were translated to English by one of the volunteers. Through Rosa, Mary was giving advise for the month of June. As usual, Mary requested that the people, to whom She referred to as her children, should pray to God and her Son. She warned that all should be aware of the economic hardships that would take place, and also predicted some problems with the weather. She cautioned the pilgrims to vote for the presidential candidate most devoted to Christianity, and not for the anti-Christ, since that would precipitate some riots and unrest in the country. She also warned that several international conflicts would take place in the near future.

The next section of the gathering was devoted to healing: Rosa gave every pilgrim a healing by the laying of hands, assisted by some of her trained volunteers. I also witnessed Rosa perform several miraculous cures on the people with serious illnesses. It was clear to me that something was happening to these patients; they could get out of their wheel chairs and start walking, shaking as they took small steps, breathing becoming more normal and assuring as their walk continued; their pains, they proclaimed, were gone. Rosa told the audience that the conditions of the patients would continue to improve, since the cures would be completed within the span of three days. After receiving my treatment as she laid her hands on the top of my head, I could feel a surge of energy inside my body. I wondered what exactly did take place, and what kind of mysterious new energy was flowing through me. I was sure that some positive change within my body occurred, and decided to monitor my well being for the next three days. The event was concluded with more prayers and chanting of Ave Maria. As Rosa exited the garden, the pilgrims started to scatter, many of them returning inside the house, hoping to get more beneficial effects of this monthly event. Earlier, one of the pilgrims gifted us with rosaries: mine was white, and Charles' was blue. They were made of synthetic material and were very sturdy, ready to last through many Ave Maria prayers. As I was looking at my gift, I realized that I forgot to observe the sky for the clouds forming unusual images, and the Sun for any visible gyration or motion. I did recall that two birds appeared in the tree nearby, and were cheerfully singing during the entire span of Rosa's trance. My experience did not seem to answer all the questions, but it was clear to me that, although filtered through Rosa's personal experience with Christianity, a contact was definitely made with some energy, or a spiritual realm. Rosa's dedication and desire to help others were obvious, and the benefits to the crowd were positive.

There was no need for a person to understand this phenomenon in order to benefit from it. The Virgin was perceived as the Mother of Humanity, loving and powerful. The organization behind Rosa Lopez, called *Our Loving Mother's Foundation*, issues a monthly newsletter to the followers. Messages from Our Mother Mary, through Rosa's interpretations, tell the followers how important small towns and average people are to the Mother and that they, rather than the powerful, need Her help the most. The messages from the Virgin assure the pilgrims how much She and her Son Jesus love them, and that they are all precious to her. They tell the crowds that Mary and Jesus ultimately are one and the same, and they walk together to bring love and compassion to all, and to disarm or neutralize everything that is evil. In so many different sentences the messages from Our Mother are about the triumph of good over evil, and although Christianity is constantly emulated, ultimately the message can be understood as the unity of female and male spirituality within one divinity. I propose that to the Christian people the message has to come in a form of a language and philosophy that is understood by the followers to facilitate the acceptance of the divine help that is reaching toward them.

Psychic phenomena are often believed to be imbued with spirituality and to have healing purposes. Prominent and small town psychics serve an important role in many people's lives; many of them publish dozens of books on self-help and spiritual philosophies of life. These usually have strong female orientations, as most psychics are involved with the issues of the divine feminine. God the Mother figures much more prominently than God the Father of the establishment among the spiritual communities. Others accept multiple aspects of the Great Mother embodied in different goddesses, and believe in super human beings living in another dimensions, such as fairies and angels. The majority of the psychics happen to be female and have an extensive following, particularly among women. These people often regard the psychic phenomena as a part of their personal religion, called Spiritualism. One of the oldest locations for the Spiritualism movement is located in Lily Dale in the state of New York; this community of Spiritualists was established in 1879 and is the largest center for the Spiritualist religion and development in America. In the state of Florida, there is a town called Cassadaga, originally founded in 1894 as a winter location for Lily Dale. Today it houses the largest group of Spiritualists within the state. Its main industry, psychic readings, attracts tourism all year round. Psychic healing, as usual, is one of the main purposes why tourists visit the city. Another is to glimpse into their personal future, or into the future world events. Others seek to communicate with their beloved family members that have departed to the other side. Special training is offered at Cassadaga that can teach a regular person to connect with the spiritual realm, and if they wish, become a part of their community as another psychic practitioner.

The psychics believe that all of us have a Goddess/God within, and that we are capable of developing extra sensory abilities that may enable us to deal with our own healings and other important situations in life that usually elicit praying from people who were raised within the contemporary society. Many of them profess to be a part of Wicca, a religion that encourages all the adepts and practitioners to develop their own psychic skills. They also emphasize that the Great Goddess, loving and compassionate, does not require that one has to suffer here on earth in order to qualify for the hypothetical heavenly realm. The Pagan religions revere the earthly as much as they do the spiritual existence therefore the idea of the planet Earth as a place for the punishment of human beings is obsolete to them. Many of the Goddess worshipers are strongly tied to various shamanic traditions that stem from old Europe and other continents, including the Native American cultures of North, Central, or South America. It is not uncommon to encounter Wiccan and other practitioners of female spirituality who received years of shamanic training and who pass their craft to others. Francesca De Grandis is such a person. In her book, *Goddess Initiation*, De Grandis explains her brand of Celtic shamanism:

"Some people believe that depth in Goddess Spirituality can be demonstrated only through theory or academically based analysis. *Goddess Initiation* will contribute an alternative view: that true depth of Goddess Spirituality can also be found through daily practice, much like the richest kernels of Buddhism. In fact the Buddha refused to discuss theology or cosmology with his students."[62]

The Americans, across the country, are experiencing a radical mind change away from traditional spirituality that requires one to respect and obey a powerful male God. He asks for submission to his will, and a deviation from his rules is followed by a punishment of the proverbial hell. This God disapproves of other gods, particularly the ones of female gender. The Mother Goddess is, on the contrary, compassionate, forgiving, and loving. The Goddess does not care if her followers also worship a male God. This inclusive spirituality is attractive to people of the new millennium, since it is flexible and includes ways by which a person may evolve within a chosen religious philosophy. Our current predominant philosophical view of the world is that of a constant change. Therefore, it is reasonable to assume that a static, immutable, and permanent deity did not create our changing universe. Instead, there is a divine force or energy that is constantly in flux, morphing and co-creating. This divinity is within everything, changing, while co-creating a multiversal reality that is constantly evolving. We recognize many convenient forms of visualizing the divine: as a female, a male, or an animal, such as the dove as a symbol for the Holy Spirit within Christianity. The nature of human thinking is symbolic, mythological, and archetypal.

The female face of God manifests herself in many different ways in America, enriched by our diverse traditions. Her temple may be a small makeshift altar in a home, a special place in the woods or in the desert. She may be invoked by a lake, on the beach, in a church, or on a visit to a temple, a museum, or even at the feet of a world famous giant statue. Her followers, pilgrims, and practitioners are scattered all over the country, and are often invisible. Some know many of their kind, while others usually worship or meditate alone. Yet others are practicing openly, no longer afraid of persecution. The embrace of the Goddess, regardless which name we may give her, is an act that is beneficial to all humanity. Whether perceived as the Holy Spirit or as Mother Earth, she is everywhere – within us, in nature, the animals, the deep of the oceans, the darkness of the soil, the air and the clouds, the sunsets, the moonlit sky, and in the energy that binds together the entire multiverse.

Bibliography

Adler, Margot. *Drawing Down the Moon*. New York: Penguin, 1986.
Allen, Paula Gunn. *Grandmothers of the Light*. Boston: Beacon Press, 1991.
_____. *The Sacred Hoop*. Boston: Beacon Press, 1992.
Anderson, Sherry Ruth & Hopkins, Patricia. *The Feminine Face of God*. New York: Bantam Books, 1991.
Ardinger, Barbara. *Goddess Meditations*. Saint Paul: Llewellyn Publications, 1998.
Ashe, Geoffrey. *The Virgin*. London: Arkana, 1988.
Awiakta, Marilou. *Selu Seeking the Corn Mother's Wisdom*. Golden: Fulcrum, 1993.
Baring, Anne and Cashford, Jules. *The Myth of the Goddess*. London: Viking Arkana, 1991.
Belan, Kyra. *Madonnas: From Medieval to Modern*. New York: Parkstone, 2001.
Berger, Pamela. *The Goddess Obscured*. Boston: Beacon Press, 1985.
Bernstein, Dan. *Secrets of the Code*. New York: CDS, 2004.
Bernstein, Dan and De Keijzer, Arnie J. *Secrets of Mary Magdalene*. Cambridge: CDS, 2006.
Blofeld, John. *Boddhisattva of Compassion*. Boston: Shambhala, 1988.
Blavatsky, H.P. *Isis Unveiled*. 2 vol. Pasadena: Theosophical Univ. Press, 1988.
Bolen, Jean Shinoda. *Goddesses in Everywoman*. San Francisco: Harper & Row, 1984.
_____. *Goddesses in Older Women*. New York:Quill, 2002.
Brading, D.A. *The Mexican Phoenix*. Cambridge: Cambridge Univ. Press, 2001.
Budapest, Zjuzjanna. *The Holy Book of Women's Mysteries*. San Francisco: Weiser Books. 2007.
_____. *The Holy Book of Women's Mysteries*. Berkeley: Wingbow Press, 1989.

Cabot, Laurie with Mills, Jean. *The Witch in Everywoman*. New York: Delta, 1997.

Canizares, Raul. *Cuban Santeria*. Rochester: Destiny, 1999.

Christ, Carol P. *She Who Changes*.New York: Palgrave Macmillan, 2003.

Castillo, Ana, ed. *Goddess of the Americas*. New York: Riverhead Books, 1996.

Condren, Mary. *The Serpent and the Goddess*. San Fransico: Harper & Row, 1989.

Cunneen, Saslly. *In Search of Mary*. New York: Ballantine Books, 1996.

Daly, Mary. *Gyn/Ecology*. Boston: Beacon Press, 1990.

_____. *Pure Lust*. Bosotn: Beacon Press, 1984.

De Grandis, Francesca. *Goddess Initiation*. San Francisco: HarperSanFrancisco, 2001.

Devine, Mary. *Magic From Mexico*. St. Paul: Llevellyn Publ., 2001.

Eisler, Riane. *The Chalice and the Blade*. San Francisco: Harper & Row, 1987.

Farrar, Janet and Stewart. *The Witches' Goddess*. Custer: Phoenix Publ., 1987.

Forrest. M. Isidora. *Isis Magic*. St. Paul: Llewellyn Publ., 2001.

Fox, Matthew. *Illuminations of Hildegard of Bingen*. Rochester: Bear & Company, 2002.

Hooper, Richard J. *The Crucifiction of Mary Magdalene*. Sedona: Sanctuary Publ., 2005.

Galland, China. *Longing for Darkness*. New York: Penguin Arcana, 1990.

Gardner, Laurence. *The Magdalene Legacy*. London: Element, 2005.

Gimbutas, Marija. *The Goddesses and Gods of Old Europe*. Berkeley: Univ. of California Press, 1982.

_____. *The Language of the Goddess*. New York: Harper & Row, 1989.

_____. *The Civilization of the Goddess*. San Francisco: HarperCollins, 1991.

Glassman, Sallie Ann. *Voodou Visions*. New York: Villard Books, 2000.

Grimassi, Raven. *Wiccan Magic*. St. Paul: Llewellyn, 1999.

Hanut, Eryk. *The Road to Guadalupe*. New York: Jeremy P. Tarcher/Putnam, 2001.

Hawley, John S. and Wulff, Donna M. *Devi*. Berkeley: Univ. of California Press,1996.

Hooper, Richard J. *The Crucifiction of Mary Magdalene*. Sedona: Sanctuary Publ.,2005.

Houston, Siobhan. *Invoking Mary Magdalene*. Boulder: Sounds True, Inc., 2006.

Jay, Roni. The Book of Goddesses. London: Darron's, 2000

Jennings, Victoria. *God as Mother*. Innersearch Books, 2002.

Johnsen, Linda. *The Living Goddess*. Saint Paul: Yes International Publ., 1999.

Jordan, Michael. *The Historical Mary*. Berkeley: Seastone, 2003.

Kanta, Katherine G. *Eleusis*. Athens: Kanta, 1979.

Kindler, Babaji Bob. *The Ten Divine Articles of Sri Durga*. Portland: SRV Oregon, 1995

King, Karen L. *The Gospel of Mary Magdalene*. Santa Rosa: Polebridge Press, 2003..

Kinsley, David. *The Goddesses' Mirror*. New York: State Univ. of New Work Press, 1989.

Kinsley, David R. *Hindu Goddesses*. Berkeley: Univ. of California Press, 1988.

Leloup, Jean-Ives. *The Gospel of Mary Magdalene*. Rochester: Inner Traditions, 2002.

Lester, Meera. *The Everything Mary Magdalene Book*. Avon: Adams Media, 2006.

Leviton, Richard. *Signs of the Earth*. Charlottsville: Hampton Roads, 2005.

Lovelock, James E. *Gaia: A New Look at Life on Earth*. New York: Oxford Univ. Press, 1991.

Luke, Helen M. *Woman Earth and Spirit*. New York: Crossroads, 1989.

Matthews, Caitlin. *Sophia Goddess of Wisdom*. London: Thorsons, 1992.

_____. *Sophia*. Wheaton: Quest Books, 2001.

Markale, Jean. *The Great Goddess*. Rochester: Inner Traditions, 1999.

Mascetti, Manuela Dunn. *The Song of Eve*. New York: Fireside, 1990.

McColman, Carl. *Embracing Jesus and the Goddess*. Gloucester: Fair Winds Press, 2001.

McCoy, Edain. *Celtic Women's Spirituality*. St. Paul: Llewellyn Publ., 1998.

McDermott, Rachel Fell and Kripel, Jeffrey J, ed. *Encountering Kali*. Berkeley: University of California Press, 2003.

McLean, Adam. *The Triple Goddess*. Grand Rapids: Phones Press, 1989.

McGrath, Sheena. *The Sun Goddess*. London: Blandford, 1997.

Mead, G. R. S. *Pistis Sophia: A Gnostic Gospel*. San Diego: The Book Tree, 2003.

Meyer, Marvin with de Boer, Esther. *The Gospels of Mary*. San Francisco: HarperSanFrancisco, 2006.

Monaghan, Patricia. *The Goddess Path*. St. Paul: Llewellyn Publ., 1999.

_____. *The New Book of Goddesses & Heroines*. St Paul: Llevellyn Publ., 2000.

Mookerjee, Ajit. *Kali The Feminine Force*. New York: Destiny Books, 1988.

Moreno, Barry. *The Statue of Liberty Encyclopedia*. New York: Simon & Shuster, 2000.

Nickel, Joe. *Looking for a Miracle*. Amherst: Prometheus Books, 1998.

Noble, Vicki. *The Double Goddess*. Rochester: Bear & Company, 2003.

Olsen, Carl, ed. *The Book of the Goddess Past and Present*. New York: Crossroads, 1994.

Patai, Raphael. *The Hebrew Goddess*. Detroit, Wayne State University Press, 1990.

Picknett, Lynn and Prince, Clide. *The Templar Revelation*. New York: Touchstone, 1998.

Picknett, Lynn. *Mary Magdalene*. New York: Carroll 7 Graf Publishers, 2004.

Pollack, Rachel. *The Body of the Goddess*. London: Vega, 2003.

Regula, deTracy. *The Mysteries of Isis*. St. Paul: Llevellyn Publ., 1995

Roberts, Alyson. *Hathor Rising*. Rochester: Inner Traditions International, 1997.

Rodriguez, Jeannette. *Our Lady of Guadalupe*. Austin: University of Texas Press, 1994.

Rose, Sharron. *The Path of the Priestess*. Rochester: Inner Traditions, 2002.

Ruether, Rosemary Radford. *Womanguides*. Boston: Beacon Press, 1985.

Sahtouris, Elizabeth. *Gaia The Human Journey From Chaos to Cosmos*. New York: PocketBooks. 1989.

Silko, Lesley Marmon. *Yellow Woman and a Beauty of the Spirit*. New York: Touchstone, 1996.

Spretnak. Charlene. *Missing Mary*. New York: Palgrave MacMillan, 2004.

Starbird, Margaret. *The Woman with the Alabaster Jar*. Rochester: Bear & Company, 1993.

_____. *The Goddess in the Gospels*. Santa Fe: Bear & Company, 1998.

_____. *Magdalene's Lost Legacy*. Santa Fe: Bear & Company, 2003.

_____. *Mary Magdalene, Bride in Exile*. Santa Fe: Bear & Company, 2005.

Starhawk. *The Spiral Dance*. San Francisco: Harper & Row, 1979.

_____. *The Earth Path*. San Francisco: HarperSanFrancisco, 2005.

Stone, Merlin. *When God Was a Woman*. New York: Harcourt Brace Jovanovich, 1976.

Teish, Luisah. *Jambalaya*. San Francisco: Harper & Row, 1985.

Telesco, Patricia. *Advanced Wicca*. New York: Citadel Press, 2000.

Waldherr, Kris. *The Book of Goddesses*. New York: Abrams, 2006.

Ward, Martha. *Voodoo Queen*. Jackson: University Press of Mississippi, 2004.

Walker, Barbara G. *The Woman's Encyclopedia of Myths and Secrets*. San Francisco: Harper & Row, 1983.

Walker, Benjamin. *Tantrism*. Wellingborough: The Aquarian Press, 1982.

Warner, Marina. *Alone of All Her Sex*. New York: Vintage Books, 1988.

Warren-Clarke, Ly. *The Way of the Goddess*. Dorset: Prism Press, 1987.

Weible, Wayne. *Medjugorje The Message*. Orleans: Parachutte Press, 1989.

Wicker, Christine. *Lily Dale*. San Francisco: HarperSanFrancisco, 2003.

Wilshire, Donna. *Virgin Mother Crone*. Rochester: Inner Traditions, 1994.

Witt, R.E. *Isis in the Ancient World*. Baltimore: The Johns Hopkins Univ. Press, 1997.

Woodman, Marion and Dickson, Elinor. *Dancing in the Flames*. Boston: Shambala, 1997.

Notes

1. Hanut, Eryk. *The Road to Guadalupe*. (New York, Jeremy P. Tharcher/Putnam, 2001), p. 30.
2. Ibid., p. 31.
3. Devine, Mary. *Magic From Mexico*. (St. Paul, Llewellyn Publ., 1992), p. 6.
4. Ibid., p. 7.
5. Rodriguez, Jeanette. *Our Lady of Guadalupe*. (Austin, University of Texas Press, 1994), p. 155.
6. Moreno, Barry. *The Statue of Liberty Encyclopedia*. (New York, Simon and Shuster, 2000), p. 74.
7. Ibid., p. 119.
8. Ibid., p. 145.
9. Walker, Barbara G. *The Woman's Encyclopedia of Myths and Secrets*. (San Francisco, Harper & Row, 1983), p. 453.
10. McGrath, Sheena. *The Sun Goddess*. (London, Blandford, 1997), p. 31.
11. Ibid., p. 91.
12. Information on the Nashville Parthenon may be found on http://www.nashville.gov/Parks-and-Recreation/Parthenon.aspx
13. Kanta, Katherine G. *Eleusis*. (Athens, 1979), p. 56.
14. Ibid., p. 57.
15. Walker, Barbara G. *The Woman's Encyclopedia of Myths and Secrets*. (San Francisco, Harper & Row, 1983), p. 453.
16. Witt, R.E. *Isis in the Ancient World*. (Baltimore, The Johns Hopkins University Press, 1997), p. 130.
17. Regula, deTraci. *The Mysteries of Isis*. (St. Paul, Llewellyn Publications, 1995), p. 133.

18. Roberts, Alyson. *Hathor Rising*. (Rochester, Inner Traditions International, 1997), p. 44.
19. Monaghan, Patricia. *The New Book of Goddesses and Heroines*. (St. Paul, Llewellyn Publications, 2000), p.185.
20. Ibid., p. 185.
21. Blofeld, John. *Bodhisattva of Compassion*. (Boston, Shambala, 1988), p. 71.
22. Boucher, Sandy. *Discovering Kuan Yin, Buddhist Goddess of Compassion*. (Boston, Beacon Press, 1999), p. 51.
23. Olsen, Carl, editor. *The Book of the Goddess, Past and Present*. (New York, Crossroads, 1994), p.170.
24. Walker, Barbra G. *The Woman's Encyclopedia of Myths and Secrets*. (San Francisco, Harper & Row, 1983), p. 976.
25. Galland, China. *Looking for Darkness: Tara and the Black Madonna*. (New York, Penguin Arkana, 1990), p. 100.
26. Mookerjee, Ajit. *Kali The Feminine Force*. (New York, Destiny Books, 1988), p. 16.
27. Ibid., p. 16.
28. Ibid ., p. 41.
29. Walker, Barbara G. *The Woman's Encyclopedia of Myths and Secrets*. (San Francisco, Harper & Row, 1983), p. 489.
30. Ibid., p. 489.
31. Ibid., p. 490.
32. Kinsley, David. *The Goddesses' Mirror*. (New York, State University of New York Press, 1989), p. 4.
33. Walker, Barbara G. *The Woman's Encyclopedia of Myths and Secrets*. (San Francisco, Harper & Row, 1983), p. 491.
34. Kinsley, David. *The Goddesses' Mirror*. (New York State University of New York Press, 1989), p. 56.
35. Waldherr, Kris. The Book of Goddesses.(New York, Abrams, 2006), p. 95.
36. Mac Gaa, Ed. *Mother Earth Spirit* (SanFrancisco,HarperSanFrancisco,1990), p. 6.
37..Waldherr, Kris. *The Book of Goddesses*. (New York, Abrams, 2006), p. 135.
38. Ibid., p.135.
39. Allen, Paula Gunn. *The Sacred Hoop*. (Boston, Beacon Press, 1992), p. 19.
40. _____. *Grandmothers of the Light*. (Boston, Beacon Press, 1991), p.33.
41. Silko, Leslie Marmon. *Yellow Woman and a Beauty of the Spirit*. (New York, Touchstone, 1996). P. 49.
42. Ibid, p. 50.
43. Burnstein, Dan. *Secrets of The Code*. (Cambridge, CDS, 2004), p.5.
44. Picknett, Lynn and Prince, Clyde. *The Templar Revelation*. (New York, Touchstone, 1988), p. 256.
45. Ibid., p. 255.
46. Gardner, Lawrence. *The Magdalene Legacy*. (London, Element, 2005), p. 140.
47. Ibid., p. 452.
48. Patai. Raphael. *The Hebrew Goddess*. (Detroit, Wayne State University Press, 1990), p. 98.

49. Teish, Luisah. *Jambalaya*. (San Francisco, Harper & Row, 1985), p. 54.
50. Ibid., p. 43.
51. Canizares, Raul. *Cuban Santeria*. (Rochester, Destiny, 1999), p. 38.
52. Ibid., p. 30.
53. Teish, Luisah. *Jambalaya*. (San Francisco, Harper & row, 1985), p. 128.
54. Ibid., P. 108.
55. Starhawk. *The Earth Path*. (San Francisco, HarperSanFrancisco, 2005), p.70.
56. _____. *The Spiral Dance*. (San Francisco, Harper & Row, 1979), p. 14.
57. Walker, Barbara G. *The Women's Encyclopedia of Myths and Symbols*. (San Francisco, Harper & Row, 1083), p. 234.
58. Sahtouris, Elizabeth. *Gaia the Human Journey From Chaos to Cosmos*. (New York, Pocket Books, 1989), p. 15.
59. Ibid., p. 15.
60. Ibid., p. 23.
61. Walker, Barbara G. The *Woman's Encyclopedia of Myths and Secrets*. (San Francisco, Harper 7 Row, 1979), p. 188.
62. De Grandis, Francesca. *Goddess Initiation*. (San Francisco, HarperSanFrancisco, 2001), p. 18.

Index

Kyra Belán

About the Author

Kyra Belán, artist, author, mythologist, and art historian,
graduated from Arizona State University with a B.F.A. in fine arts,
and from Florida State University with an M.F.A. in visual arts.
Her Ed. D., from Florida International University, is in higher education
and art history. Dr. Belán has had over 60 solo art exhibitions and has
participated in over 90 group art exhibitions. She has received numerous
awards, including Who's Who in American Art, the Florida
Achievement Award in the Arts, Women's Caucus for Art Florida Chapter,
2007-8; the Southeastern Art Conference Outstanding Artistic
Achievement Award, University of Arkansas at Little Rock 2005; Broward
County's Women's Hall of Fame Outstanding Achievement in the Arts,
1994; and the Individual Artist Fellowship, State of Florida, Florida Arts
Council. 1982. Her artworks are found in numerous public and private collections.
Author of several articles published in journals, Dr. Belán has
co-authored a book, *Dorothy Gillespie*, Radford University Press, 1998.
She has written a novel, *Lucid Future*, Aegina Press, 1999; Createspace 2014,
and a book titled *Madonnas: From Medieval to Modern*, Parkstone Press,
2001 (English, German, and French). Fifth edition of her book, *Earth, Spirit, and
Gender: Visual Language for the New Reality*, was published by Thomson; sixth and
seventh edition, titled *Art, Myths, and Rituals*, was published by Bent Tree Press in
2007 – 2010. *The Virgin in Art: From Medieval to Modern*, Barnes & Noble Books,
New York, 2006, and *La Virgen en el Arte*, Panamericana, was published in 2007.
Belan is included in *100 Contemporary International Artists*, Biblioteca de Artistas
de las Comunidades Europeas, 2007. Her new book, *Earth, Myths, and Ecofeminist
Art*, Createspace, 2015, is available on Amazon.com in paperback and kindle editions.

Dr. Belan is the Otto M. Burkhardt Endowed Chair and professor of art and art
history emerita, Broward College, Pembroke Pines Campus, and the founding art
gallery director there from 1991 to 2011; she coordinated the Seminole Arts and
Culture Project at Broward College from 2007 to 2009. Currently she is working on
her book on *Installation Art*, Mellen Press, an International Scholarly Publisher of
Advanced Research.

Kyra Belan is a frequent art exhibitor, lecturer and conference presenter, and
resides in southwest Florida with her husband and two dogs.

www.ingramcontent.com/pod-product-compliance
Lightning Source LLC
Chambersburg PA
CBHW081631040426

42449CB00014B/3263